FLORIDA ARTIST

Wᵐ North

His Life and Art

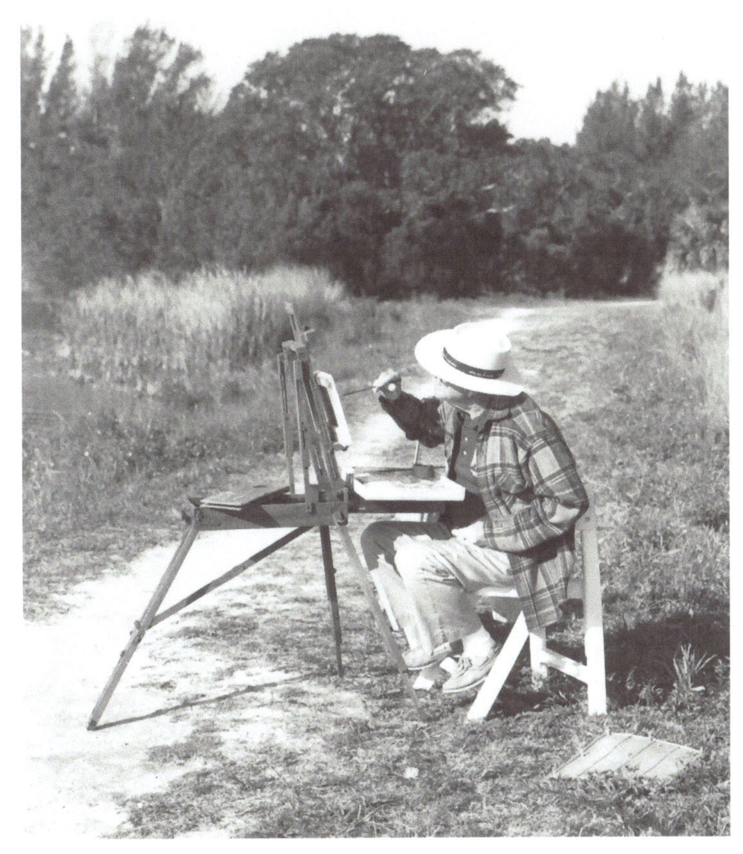

Colleen R. North
with William North

Dedications

The lucky man has a daughter as his first child.
—Spanish proverb

Dedicated to fathers and daughters, and the bond they forge.

Colleen R. North

Dedicated to my wife, Colleen Cole North, for embracing my vision and sharing my life.

William North

Cover painting: *Indigo Trail*, William North

ISBN 978-1-935751-03-8
Florida Artist: Wm. North, His Life and Art
© 2011, Colleen R. North with William North
Published by
Scribbulations LLC
PO Box 3027tcb
West Orange, NJ 07052
www.scribbulations.com
Printed in the United States of America

Acknowledgement

I would like to acknowledge the aid and skillful assistance of my publisher Ed Charlton, editor Lisa Romeo, webmaster Nancy Koucky, photographers Megan Kissinger and Mahmoud Sami, and Ludmila Evans.

A special note of appreciation to the Gannon family for their enthusiastic interest and support, and my mother and sisters for their encouragement of this family project.

Colleen R. North

www.NorthGallery.com

Contents

Introduction

My Father, the Early Years

My father, William Charles North, was only 24 years old when I was born in 1951. During my childhood and teenage years, he always seemed to me such a serious, private man, a dedicated businessman who mostly wore a suit and worked in an office, though I did notice that he was artistic too. I always felt a strong creative link between the two of us. Still, to me he was a typical Dad, successful in his job, and someone whose approval I craved. There is a portrait he painted of me in my high chair, so I know that even as a young dad, he must have found time to paint. I didn't know then of course, how much he craved to live the artist's life full time, and it seems it has taken me most of my adult life to see how similar we both are.

I'm so honored now to collaborate with my father on this account of his life as an artist, an accomplishment achieved perhaps a bit later in life than he may have wanted. Maybe that's why he savors it so. Some of the pages ahead are in his own words, based on memory and records and most of all, his love of painting.

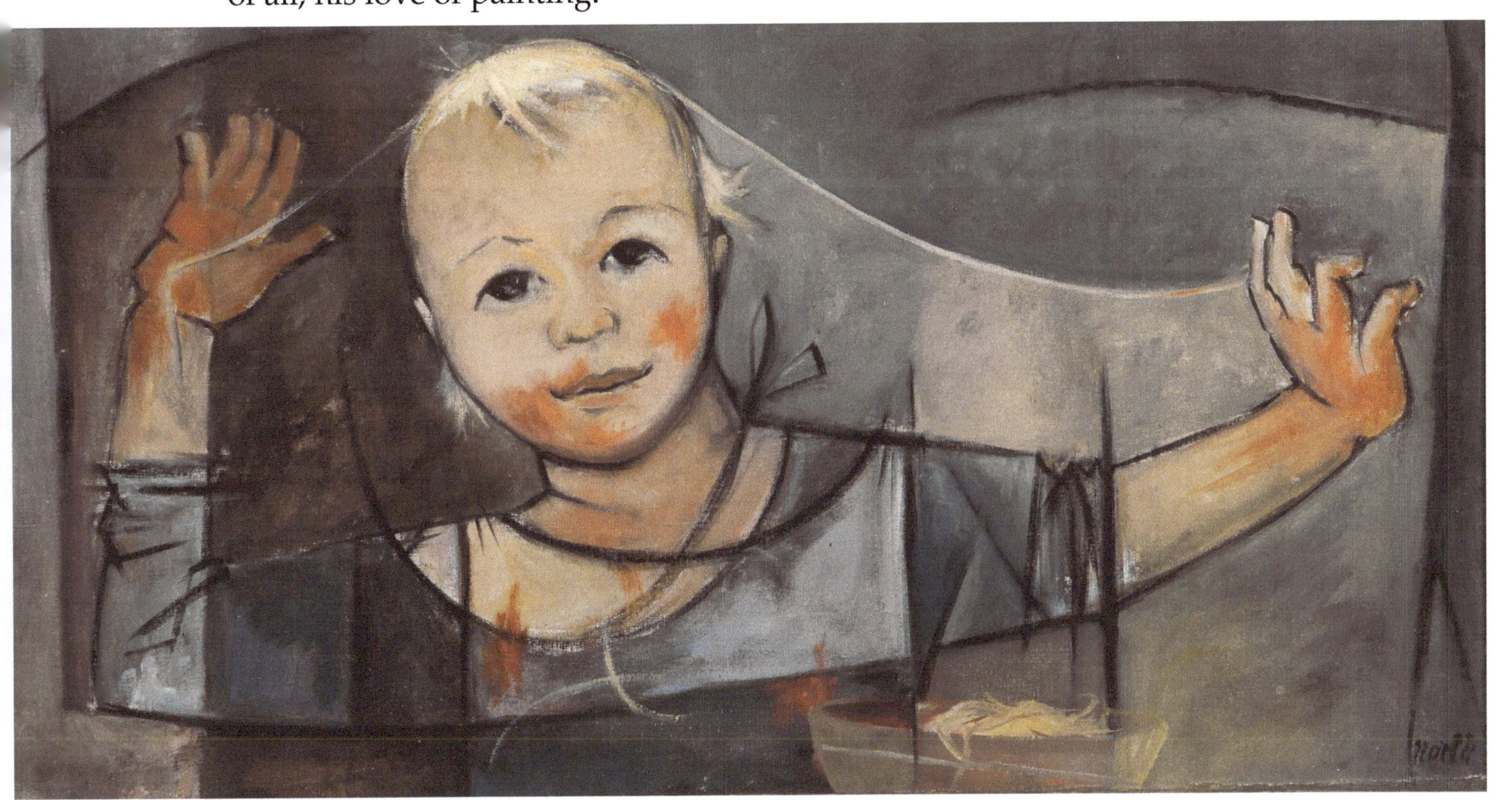

Dad painted me eating spaghetti in my highchair at age ten months.

Of course Dad's life as an artist was unfolding while I was busy living my own. Except for the first 20 years of my life when we lived under the same roof, his artistic ambitions and achievements were usually relayed to me by my mother, Colleen, his supportive wife of 62 years. I knew only that he made a living for his family working in public relations, and that he sometimes painted on weekends. It wasn't until I was in my 50's and began to put together his story for this book that I truly understood that Dad had lived a sort of double life—businessman *and* artist. He had been painting all along, it turned out, but it wasn't until he retired from the business world and devoted himself to painting full time that I took him seriously as an artist. And what an artist!

Since 1990 Dad has been a well-regarded and prolific painter in Southwest Florida, selling more than 600 original oil paintings and countless prints. His work is sold in several Florida galleries, has hung in the Governor's Gallery at the State Capitol in Tallahassee, and received numerous awards. It is included in hundreds of collections around the U.S., in Moscow and Tokyo, and he has even been named artist-in-residence at a Florida state park. He still paints nearly every day in his Florida studio, while most of the time I'm busy selling real estate in New Jersey.

Prior to 2005, Dad would have been very capable of putting his story on paper with little assistance from me. But everything changed when he began experiencing trouble with his vision and received a diagnosis that would drastically impact his world: Age-Related Macular Degeneration (AMD), a chronic disease of the eye causing a loss of central vision. While he's taught himself to continue to paint in the face of this challenge, staring at words on a computer screen was best left to someone else, to me.

To help him complete this book, I interviewed my father, many times, and through those conversations, I came to realize that Dad had always thought of himself as an artist first. Being able to paint full time was his lifelong ambition, eventually and abundantly fulfilled. As this book is printed (in early 2011), Dad is still painting at age 83, and has adapted his technique only slightly to accommodate his changed vision. From his notes and memorabilia we have collaborated to tell the story of a man who accomplished so much in his life, but who derived his greatest satisfaction by creating an oil painting from conception to completion.

During my 60 years as his first-born child, I've spent many hours with Dad, watching while he painted outdoors and in the studio. These intimate moments provided me with so many opportunities to observe how he worked and to understand his personal approach to oil painting. Usually such a quiet man, he'd open up to me when he was painting, explaining in detail what he was doing and why, and offering a few tidbits of art history or quotes from famous artists. Now, as I watch Dad adapt to his vision loss and to aging, I see that his dedication to expressing himself through oils, his success as an artist, and his pure love of creativity, all achieved at long last, will continue to hold him in good stead. There's only one sure thing in his future: more art.

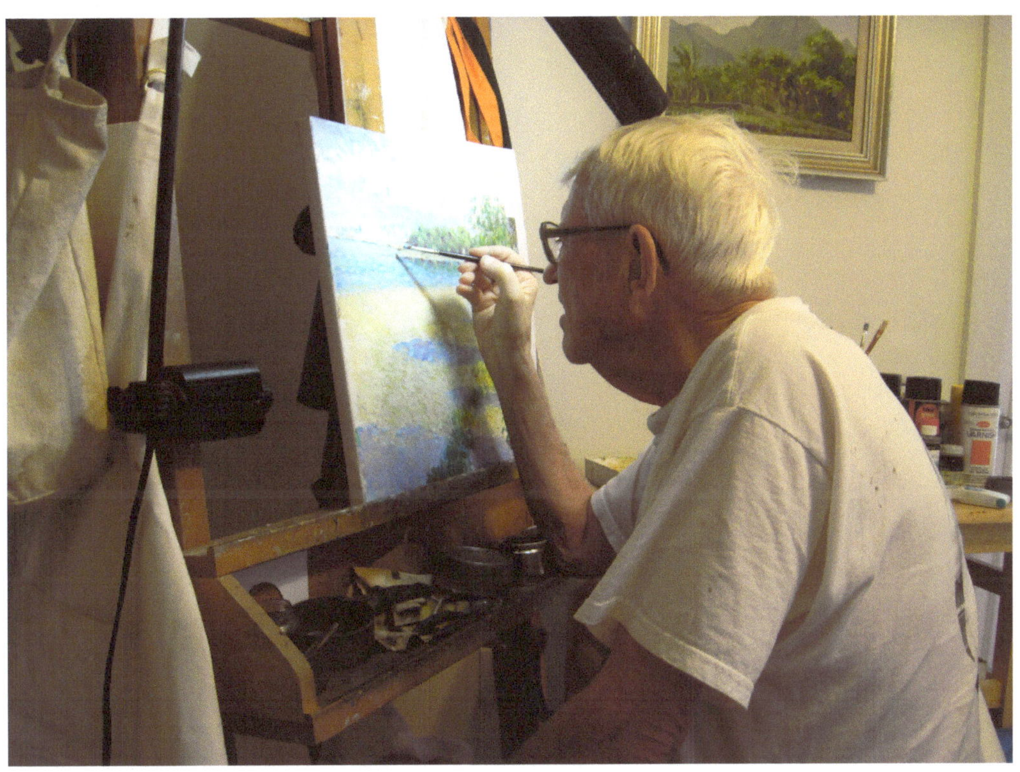

Dad at his easel in Ft. Myers, Florida.

My Father, the Artist

The Studio

Since my earliest childhood memories, Dad had a studio in our family home. As I was growing up, and our family moved from one house to the next, it seemed that his studio only grew larger. Although I took it for granted, I eventually came to realize that having a space in which to paint that felt *just right* was a desire that would never leave him.

When my parents retired and moved from New England to Florida, the studio he created in their house in Fort Myers was a grand affair. Its spacious 14 x 14 feet included wall-to-wall file drawers, storage units for art supplies, and still life props, as well as gallery-style track lighting to showcase his finished work. If he wanted a little music while he painted, his stereo set the mood as he listened to Mozart or Beethoven. During football season, the familiar play-by-play kept him abreast of the action. In Connecticut he followed the New York Giants, but when he arrived in Florida he split his loyalty between the Tampa Bay Buccaneers and the Miami Dolphins. A large studio easel occupied the center of the room, and next to the easel stood his taboret (cart with wheels), holding his palette and brushes. On another stand to the left of the easel Dad set up his still life shadow box. The studio's large window let in plenty of sunshine, and looked out at a lake where waterfowl fed. When clients or friends would visit, they could relax on the sofa and talk the business or aesthetics of painting with Dad while he worked.

Painting Outdoors

Painting indoors produced one type of work—still life, and especially those showing citrus. Dad fell in love with Florida citrus—the real, imperfect fruits found in the nearby groves, not the ones in pricey fruit baskets. But for landscapes Dad went out on location to paint en plein aire (a French expression meaning "in the open air"). These excursions involved a trip in the car to the painting site, which he carefully selected for some unique aspect—perhaps the view, or a particular type of foliage, the color of the sand, or the presence of an engaging house or other building.

Just like a hiker, Dad would carry everything necessary: an easel, large tote bag, chair and primed canvas. He used a portable French half easel, a smaller and lighter version of the full size, and wore out five of these during 30 years of location painting. Between 1990 and 2009, Dad painted outdoors nearly every day.

His final landscape painted completely on location was *Shady Trail–Wiggins Beach*, in September 2009, at Florida's Delnor-Wiggins Pass State Park in North Naples, where he had been honored as Artist-in-Residence for the 2007-8 season.

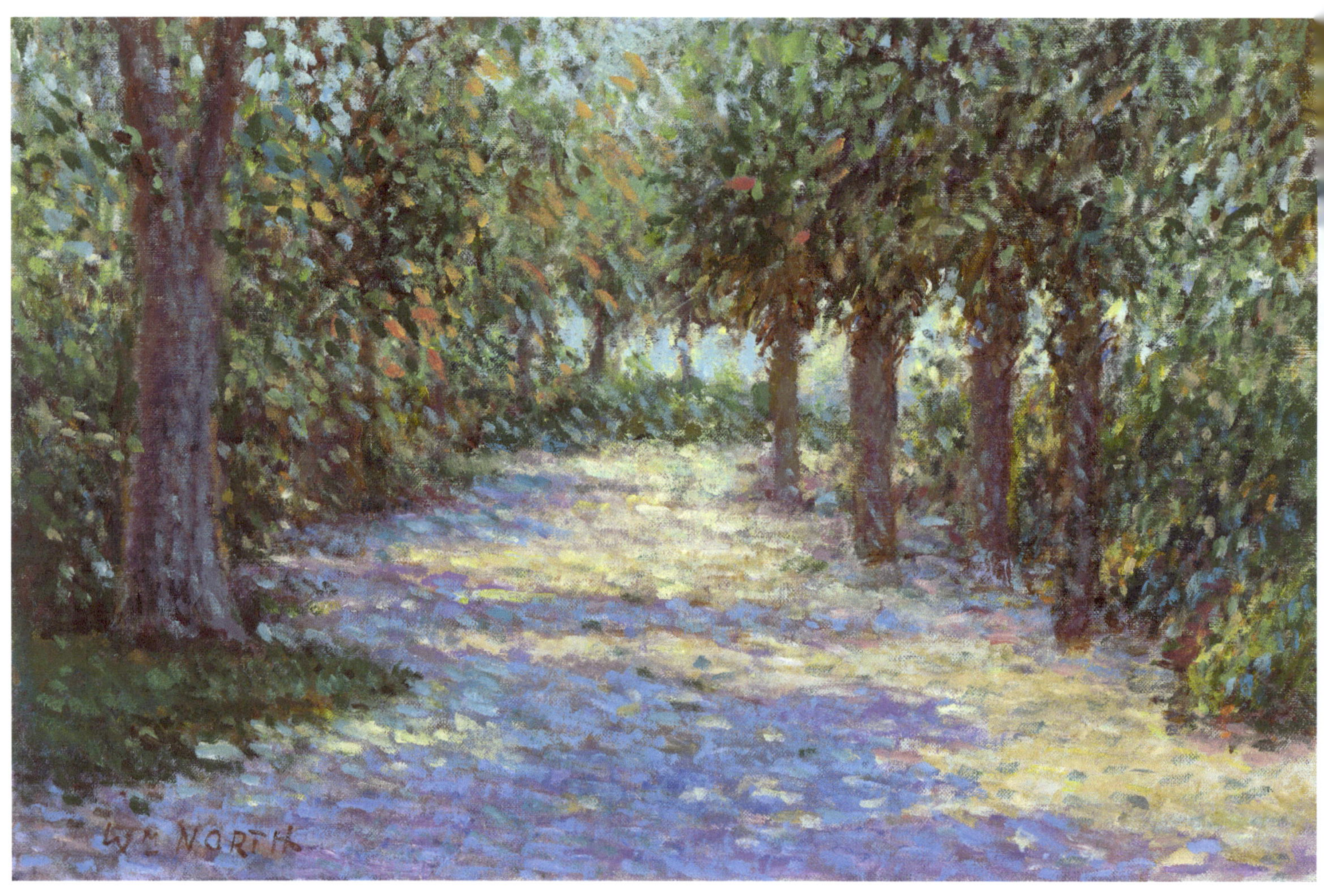

"Shady Trail–Wiggins Beach," his last painting done on location. Dad portrayed the path to the beach, but left out the Bar-B-Q facilities for aesthetic reasons. "That's called 'artistic license,'" he quipped.

Technique & Materials

From his earliest days, Dad painted only in oil, which he called the "medium of the masters." By masters he meant both the old European masters and the pioneering impressionists such as Claude Monet and Childe Hassam, and countless others around the world. He'd point out that the paintings hanging in the world's great museums are mostly oils. Edgar Degas was among his favorites, and he often quoted the artist: "Good painting consists of variety with unity."

As for his own style, Dad says he is an impressionist, and employs the elements of impressionism in his technique. These elements include use of complimentary colors and reflected light and color, loose brushwork, visible brushstrokes, appropriate handling of hard, soft and lost edges, and restrained contrast. When he began painting in Florida in 1990, many people compared him to Georges Seurat, and viewers of his work sometimes asked if his technique was pointillism because of his use of small brush strokes which resembled tiny dots. When asked about the comparison Dad said, "I take comparing my work to Seurat's pointillism as a compliment, although I don't quite see it myself."

Dad's basic palette consists of a *warm* and a *cool* of each primary color. Knowing that warm colors advance and cool colors recede, he always sets out Cadmium Yellow Medium, Cadmium Red Light, and Ultramarine Blue for warms, and Lemon Yellow or Cadmium Yellow Light, Alizarin Crimson, and Cerulean or Thalo Blue for cools. He also almost always uses three earth colors: Yellow Ochre, Raw Sienna, and Burnt Sienna; two greens: Sap Green and Chrome Oxide; and Titanium White—*and no black*. In his paintings of Florida citrus, he includes Cadmium Yellow Deep and Diazoline Purple. His goal, when he moved south from New England, was to capture the Florida sunshine and as a result most of his paintings are high key (bright and sunny).

When asked once if he changed his palette after moving to Florida, Dad answered, "No, you should be able to paint anything anywhere with a basic palette. You can't buy a tube of paint called 'tropical sky' or 'gulf blue.' But if there *are* some colors you're always mixing, and you can find it in a tube, why not just buy it?"

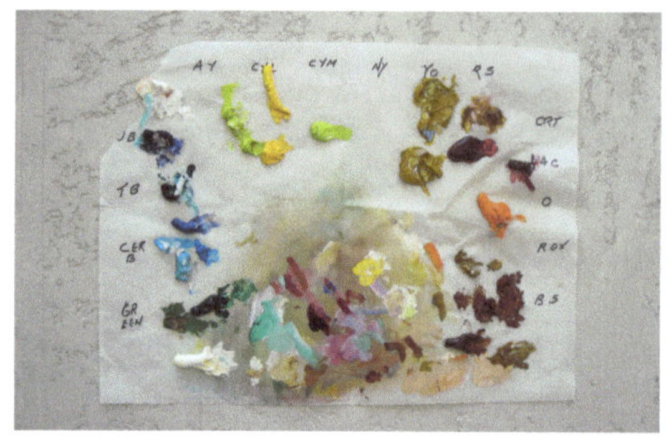

He favors a 12" x 16" paper palette stored in a Masterson airtight box. His canvas is lead primed linen Frederix Kent 125 SP (single primed). When asked about his choice of canvas material, Dad is fond of saying, "The Egyptian mummies were wrapped in linen and the fabric has lasted for thousands of years. I want my work to last."

His brushes are #1 Grumbacher Bristlette flats which produce a very small stroke. These are no longer available, but years ago he purchased a large supply that will last. Several small sable rounds are used for certain details and for signing his name. He uses cat food tins filled with turpentine, mineral spirits or turpenoid to clean his brushes, which he diligently washes in soap and water after each day's use. Another tin holds a 50/50 mixture of turps and linseed oil for thinning out paints. These are always out on the easel, ready to use, and capped with larger sized tuna tins to keep the contents from evaporating.

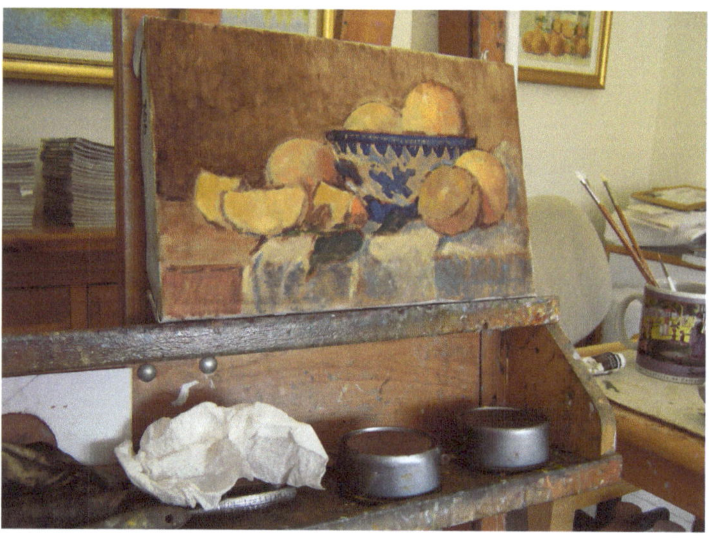

Unlike some other artists, Dad never does preliminary sketches, so there are no sketch books. Instead, he's always had a backlog of paintings in his head, and with a great feeling for composition and design, he makes his adjustments directly on the canvas as he paints. Until 2010 he stretched his own canvases to a size and proportion appropriate for his next project. Arthritis and age have taken away enough hand strength that he now uses framers for this task, delivering stretcher bars and canvas to them. His sizes range from 8" x 10" to 20" x 40".

The Artistic Process

Dad approaches a bare canvas with a piece of vine charcoal in his right hand, and a chamois in the other. With minimal drawing, just a dozen lines or so, he blocks in the composition. He says painting is full of decisions every step of the way, so when approaching a beach scene, for example, he first decides whether it is to be a sky, water, or beach painting. Then he allocates space and plans the details accordingly. Something must dominate, so after these decisions are made he draws the horizon line first, usually placed high. Next he'll place the water line and block in the other dominant shapes.

After the charcoal sketch, Dad dusts off the excess charcoal by blowing on it or by flicking the chamois. Then he does a more detailed drawing with a brush using thinned Burnt Sienna paint because it dries faster than other pigments. Once he is satisfied with the drawing, he uses an old brush to scrub in a wash of local color he calls a "ghost" or "shadow painting." Then he starts to apply paint.

Discussing the actual application of paint, Dad explains that a painting has two main elements: the pictorial and the artistic. Once he's worked out the composition (the pictorial), it's time to focus on the artistic, the feeling that goes along with the picture. As a young boy he took piano lessons, and remembers the teacher telling him, "Play it once more with feeling."

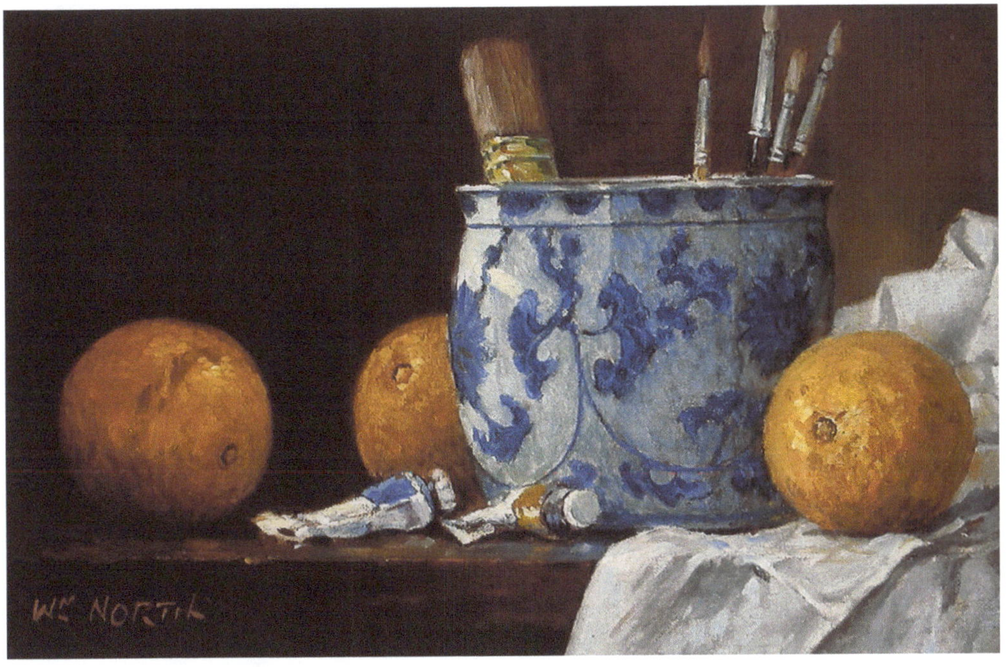

Florida Oranges in the Artist's Studio, Ft. Myers, Florida.

"In my youth I didn't know what that feeling was, but in my maturity I began to have a sense of it," he told me. "You can't achieve a feeling of artistry on your canvas by accident. The magic comes from your application of the paint." This kind of knowledge, combined with adept skill in handling the paint, allows him to achieve the artistry from his strategic placement of strokes and color.

"For the finished work, if you want your brush strokes to show, you must not paint over them," Dad notes. He usually starts painting at the place where three or more elements appear, trying to get the colors and value relationships to his liking. Then he works all over the painting, constantly modifying and correcting the drawing, color and value as he goes. "It's like modeling in clay," he says. "You add a little and take off a little until you think you have it just right." He adheres to the 'fat over lean' rule in which the earlier layers of paint are thinned only with turps and the final layers of paint have more oil, so the painting dries from bottom layer out. Dad uses this technique because he wants the work to last, and because he hopes that one day his best paintings will be highly valued.

Dad is not a member of the 'slash and parry' school of painting, nor is he a slave to the subject before him. He works methodically, putting down each brush stroke carefully. In some cases, where appropriate, he puts down thick paint, like Monet did in his cathedral series, to add texture to the architectural effect. In other cases, such as rendering a glass in a still life, he'll strive for a smoother, more polished finish. For Dad, the scene or still life arrangement is his inspiration and provides most of the detail, but he says he can also envision the finished painting in his mind, even before he starts, and he works toward that particular vision.

Deciding when a painting is finished looms with each new piece. Every artist knows that the time will come when you must decide that the work is done. However, Dad's not averse to making major changes to an almost finished work, as he once did with a red pickup truck in a scene of a citrus grove. He redrew and repainted that truck four times before he was satisfied. Dad frequently says, "Nothing is too much trouble to do it right, and impatience is the enemy of good painting."

Dad's Assistant: Mom

Painting is a solitary quest, but Dad's constant companion and biggest supporter has always been my mother, Colleen (yes, I was named after her). She was, and remains, always at his side to support him in his struggles and share in his achievements. When he works, Dad will call on Mom for a quick critique and consultation on an area of concern. She knew of his passion for painting when they met 62 years ago, and he always values her opinion. He is quick to credit her artistic sensibility, and devotion to him, for keeping his brush on the right path. To me, their example of a shared creative life has been inspiring.

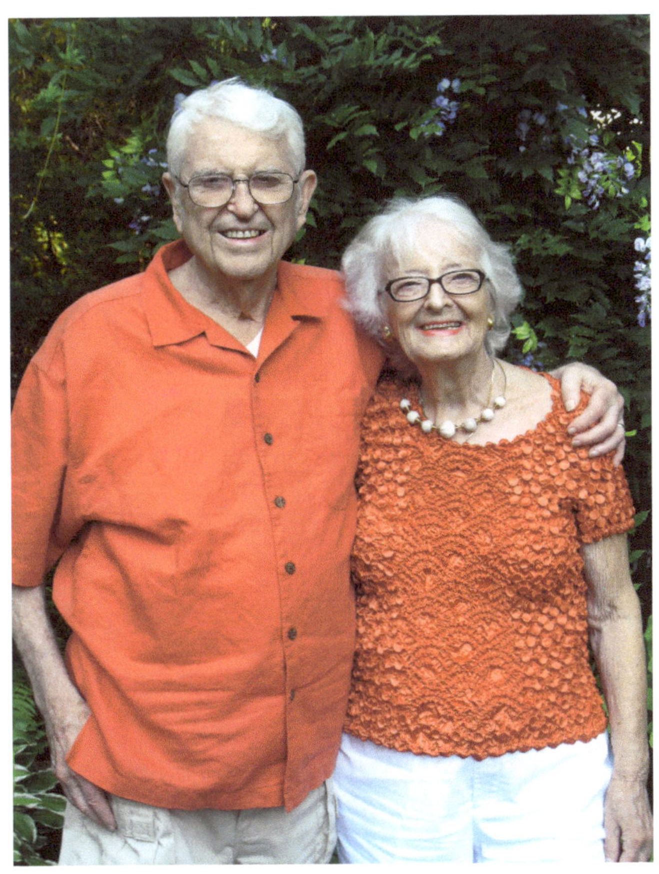

Bill and Colleen North, 60th Wedding Anniversary.

The Artist in His Own Words

Youth

I don't remember the date of my first visit to a fine art museum, but I remember the feeling. I marveled at the works hanging on the walls, produced by such painting luminaries as Claude Monet, John Singer Sargeant, Velasquez, Rembrandt and Toulouse Latrec. Even as a young boy, I was greatly impressed and felt the ambition rising in me to be a painter of works like these. That ambition has never left me. It's with me still, even at age 83.

I was born September 6, 1927, in Philadelphia. My parents, William Charles and Helen Lane North, married in the south during the Depression and were headed north in search of employment, eventually settling our family in Newark, New Jersey. There my father got a job at Breyers Ice Cream Company, where he spent his entire working life.

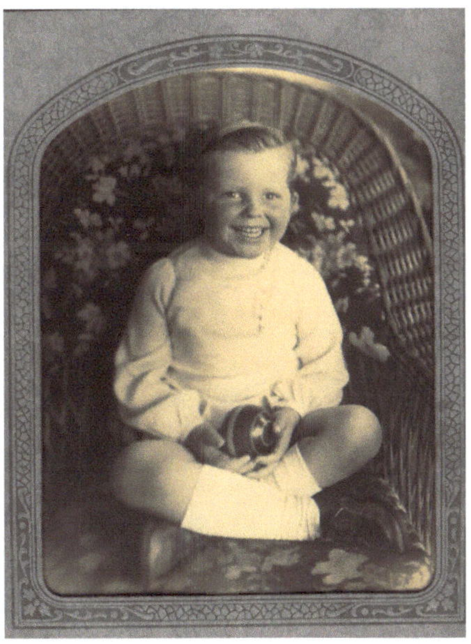

*At age 4, he didn't know the exciting life that lay ahead,
but Dad was on the ball.*

As a child I was an avid reader, and loved to draw. Too poor to have many toys, I used the few I had as models, and drew their likenesses on paper, producing handmade toy soldiers, cars, trucks and cowboys and Indians to play with. Cowboy fiction was popular, and pulp magazines for sale in every corner drug store provided images of costumes and horses and six shooters.

During the Depression we couldn't consider buying a fancy sketchpad, but I drew on scraps of paper and the cardboards that came inside Dad's shirts from the laundry. Best of all were the large paper calendar pages my father brought home from the office as each month passed. I used the backs of these to create large panoramic scenes of WWI battles in trenches, with bi-planes in the air.

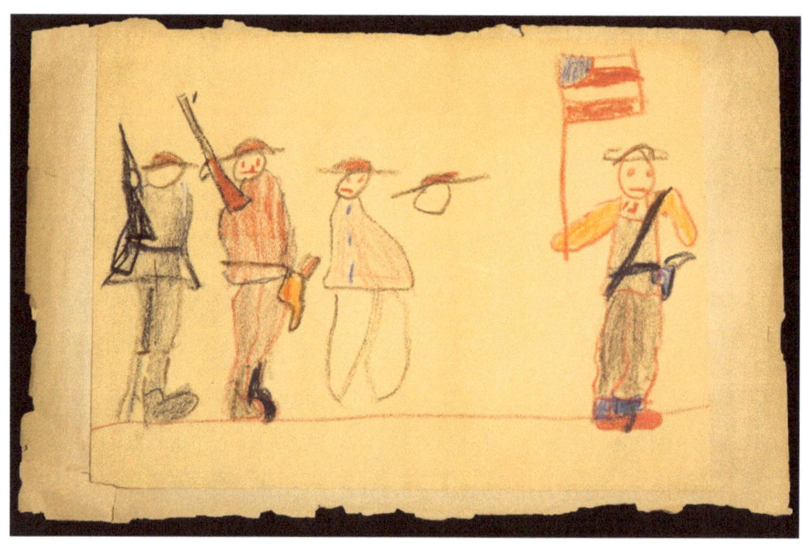

Asked when he first got interested in art, Dad usually said "before kindergarten." This drawing was done with crayons in the second grade at age seven, and saved over the years by his mother. They show his early aptitude for freehand drawing.

During my youth, I attended several schools in Newark, Clifton and Belleville, New Jersey, and continued my love of drawing. Because of a move to south Jersey, I graduated eighth grade as one of only seven in the class, in a town at the edge of the Pine Barrens called Bayville. Eventually we moved back to northern New Jersey again, and I graduated from Belleville High School. It was in this working class town that I had the good fortune to take art lessons and receive instruction in oil painting while still in high school. A truly inspired art teacher there, Paul Diehl, took an interest in motivating his handful of talented artists, and I remember being respected for my talents by other students. (Today it seems to me that high school students are only praised for talents in sports and music, and art has slid out of favor, which is too bad.) I worked on the school newspaper and capped off my high school career by designing the Class of '45 yearbook, and created the illustrations with a World War II Pacific Naval theme for the end papers and the interior section dividers.

A Military Year

Immediately after graduation I was drafted, and entered the US Army that fall, sent off to basic training in Field Artillery at Fort Bragg, North Carolina. In early 1946, I left for LeHarve, France, aboard the ship Chapel Hill Victory.

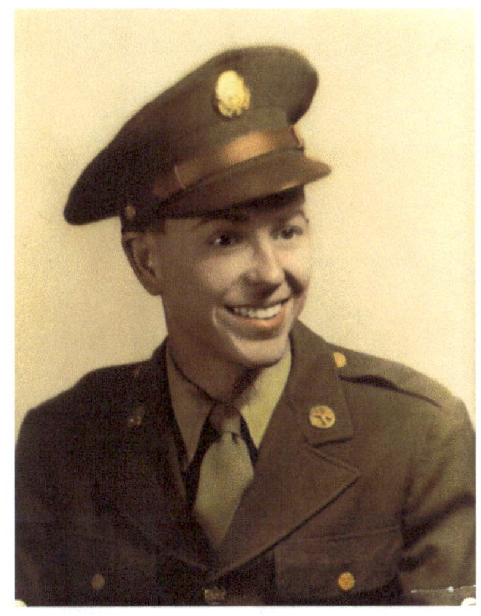

Eighteen years old and ready to serve in his new uniform with brass buttons.

My interest in art was noted in my army records, so when my personnel file was reviewed on board, I was assigned, along with a few others, to publish the ship's newspaper. Upon learning of the assignment, I remember my heart soared, and I felt an immediate improvement in my current living conditions: Working on the paper would get me out of the bowels of the ship to the upper decks where there was light and occasionally fresh air.

The paper was produced on board using old mimeo technology, and all the artwork was cut into the stencil by hand with a stylus. The image of a forlorn GI, bent over the ship's rail, was my inspiration for naming the paper *The Railbender*. Charts showing the ship's progress, and cartoons created by me, were also produced during the eleven-day voyage.

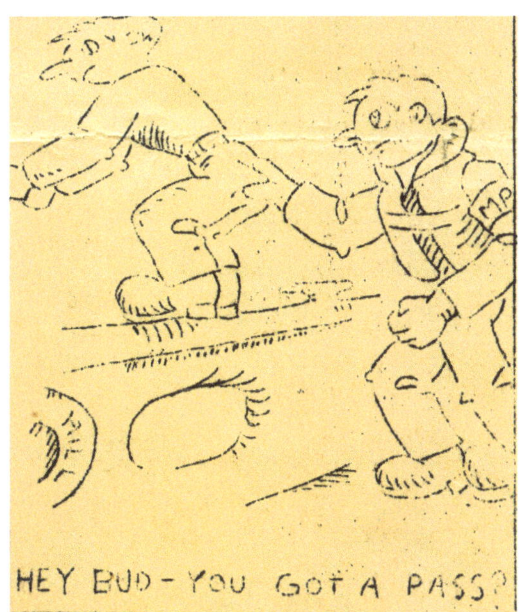

An MP checks on a seasick sailor trying to leave the ship by jumping overboard. (It didn't really happen.)

When we landed in France I was sent to Repple Depple Lucky Strike (Replacement Depot). Because of my publishing duties on board ship, I was pulled out of the field artillery, and assigned to the public relations office. First assignment was to the Seventh Army, then the Third Army and finally to the Office of Military Government for Bavaria (OMGB), where we put out a biweekly tabloid newspaper for the American troops assigned there.

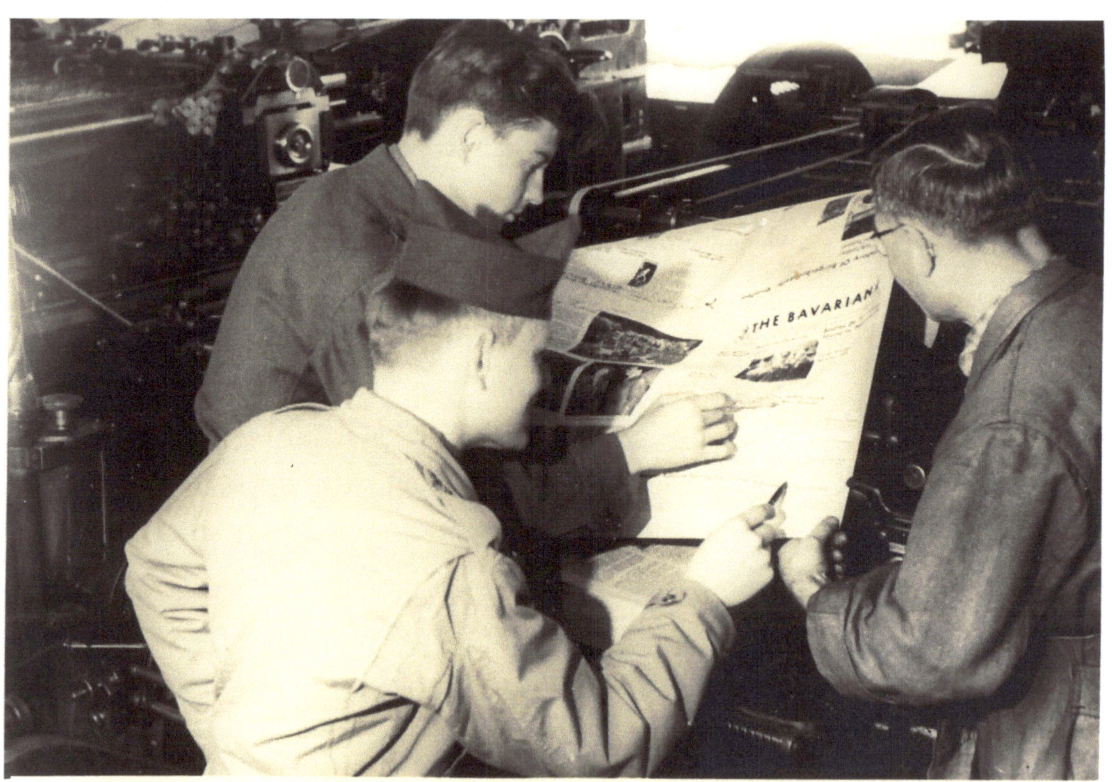

Proofreading "The Bavarian" newspaper was an ongoing challenge. The German typesetter neither spoke nor read English so it was a letter by letter, word by word process. Here, on deadline, staffers North and Lou Pica go over the proofs, taking one last look to produce a relatively typo-free paper for their fellow GI readers.

The paper was called *The Bavarian*, and along with other duties, I was the art editor. I wrote and illustrated stories, took photographs and occasionally escorted visiting civilian correspondents. On the dark side, I covered the Malmedy Trial at Dachau, where German soldiers were accused of killing captured American GIs, and reported on the recent exhumation of newly discovered concentration camp victims. On the lighter side of army life, I wrote features and human-interest stories, such as the composition of the Christmas carol, *Silent Night, Holy Night,* and the discovery of stolen art treasures.

Some assignments seemed made just for the artist in me. I illustrated life around me with spot cartoons, and co-wrote and illustrated a regular comic strip called *When Knights Were Bold,* a parody of army life loosely inspired by the campy movie *Robin Hood* starring Errol Flynn. The story line involved WWII situations with characters in medieval dress, which drew upon my practice drawing in my youth. This plum assignment meant the end of regular soldiering for me, and turned out to be a rather cushy job. A lot of pleasure was removed from it, though, when reveille was reinstated sometime in 1946, forcing me to get up at dawn with the rest of the men.

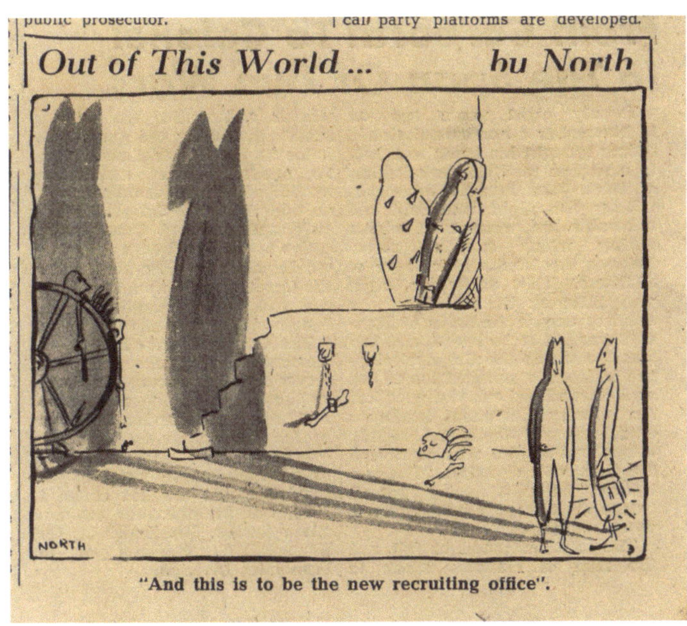

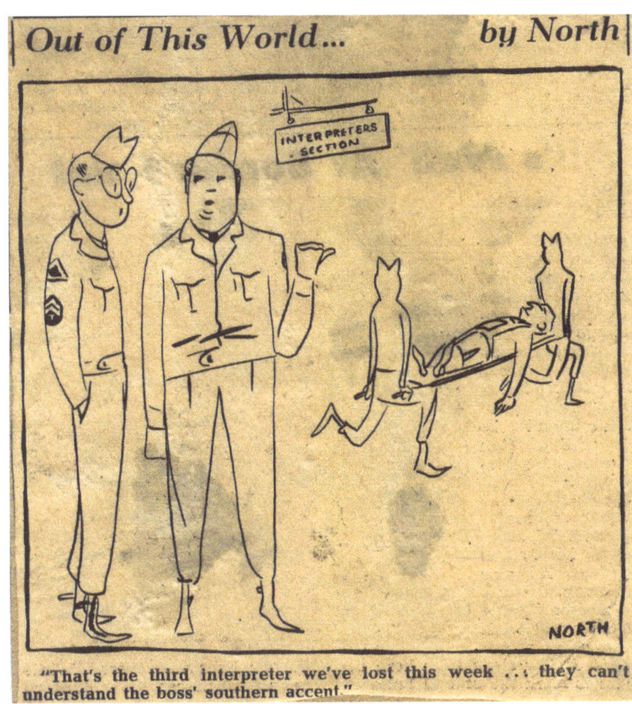

Spot cartoons were a regular feature of Dad's army newspaper. Interpreters of all nationalities were needed. Finding someone who spoke 'southern' was a challenge.

During my time overseas I was constantly drawing as part of my job, which improved my art skills considerably. In post-war Germany I was able to view recovered art, and I sought out art museums during my leave. I came home to New Jersey in 1947 aboard the Admiral Rodman, and upon return to civilian life, applied for admission to Pratt Institute in Brooklyn, and was accepted under the benefits of the GI Bill. My summer before classes began was spent working as a freelance cartoonist, submitting ideas to less-than-first-rate magazines and doing finished art work on those that were accepted. This artwork was published, but none of the magazine companies are in business today, and I fear none would look good on a resume anyway! Yet that summer contributed quite a bit to the development of my favorite activity: art.

Art College Days

Classes at Pratt Institute ran Monday through Friday, from 9 to 5. Living in Belleville, New Jersey, meant taking the train to New York's Penn Station, loaded with art student gear, and then the subway to the Pratt campus in Brooklyn. While Art Education was the only degree program offered at this fine art school, I did receive a well-rounded liberal arts education by the time I earned my BFA from Pratt in 1951.

My most lasting impression of my college days was lunch hour, when a group of us male students would retreat to the basement for lunch and to play Hearts. During my four years of Hearts I developed the skill of knowing with almost virtual certainty which cards were in which hands. I've thought about how my intuition with cards might be related to my visual acuity, and I often wondered what would have happened if I had chosen a career as a card shark!

It was during my second year at Pratt that I met and soon married a Belleville girl, Colleen Cole, who had recently graduated from Arts High School in Newark. She shared my vision of leading a creative life, and we married on July 31, 1949. The lives of young couples moved rapidly in those days, so we started our life together while I was finishing up my course work, and our first child Colleen, named after her mother, was born before my college graduation.

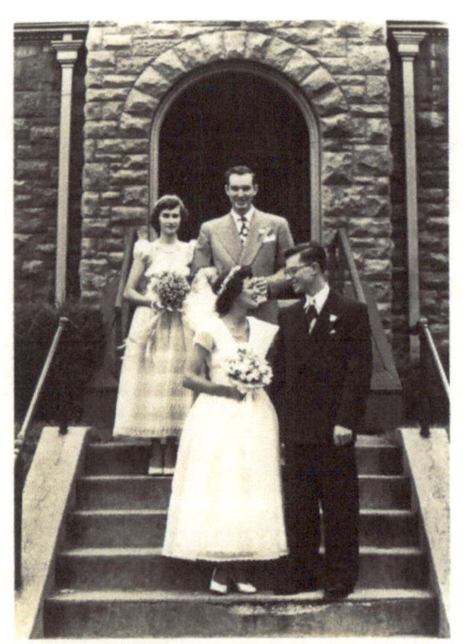

Dad with his sweetheart on their wedding day.

Artistic Inspirations, Family Obligations

Many of the artists who inspired me then were already out of favor with the public, since so-called "modern art" was currently in vogue. Realism was mostly scorned, and I felt the times were not favorable for an artist who wanted to paint in a traditional way. I also had to decide whether my family would live in a comfortable suburban split level or the garret of a starving artist. I decided to follow a traditional career path, because pursuing a job in the business world would be the best way to support our small but growing family.

Looking back I'm disappointed that I could not do more painting, but did achieve a great deal of satisfaction from putting my creativity to work in business. After college I combined my art and publication production experience, and got a job at the Mutual Benefit Life Insurance Company in Newark, as associate editor of the company newsletter, then commonly known as its 'house organ.' With a new job, new baby and the responsibilities that come with family life, I somehow still maintained a regular painting schedule on nights and on weekends.

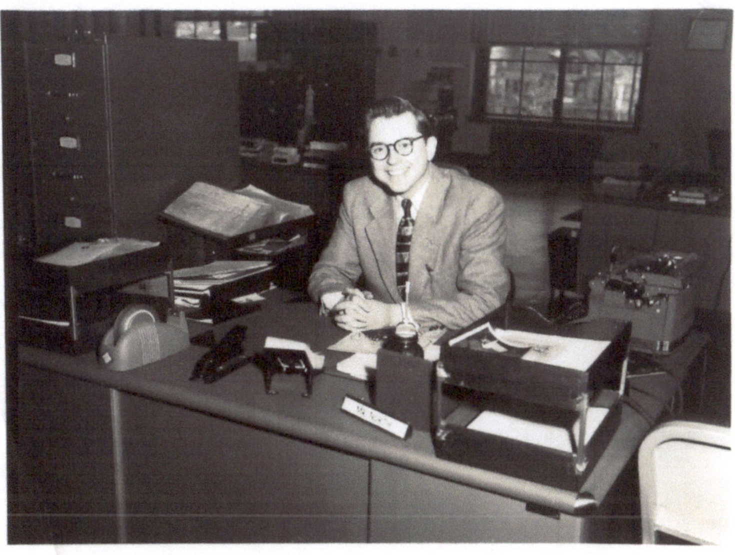

*Associate Editor, Bill North, at Mutual Benefit Life Insurance Co.
in Newark, NJ.*

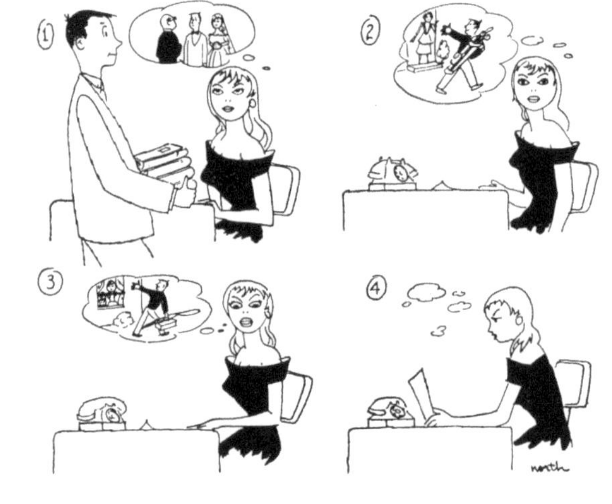

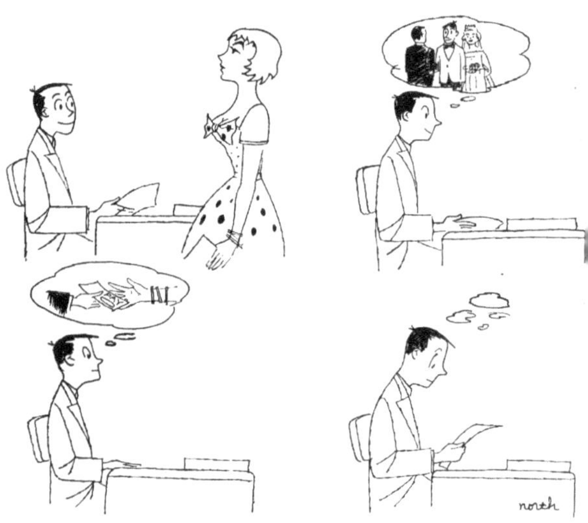

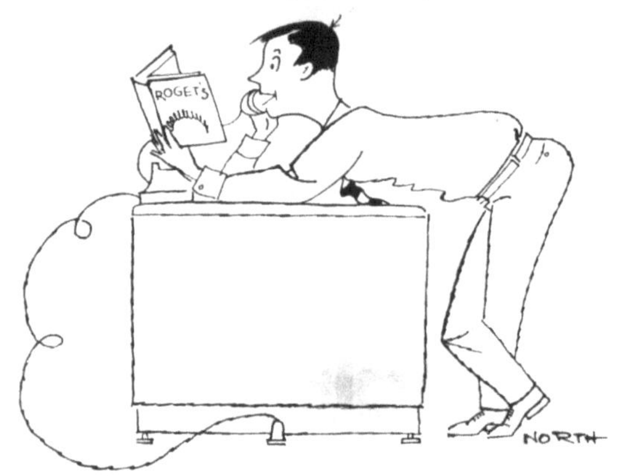

"You know I think you're lovely, adorable, sweet, winning, winsome, charming, engaging, interesting, alluring, attractive, enchanting, captivating, fascinating and bewitching."

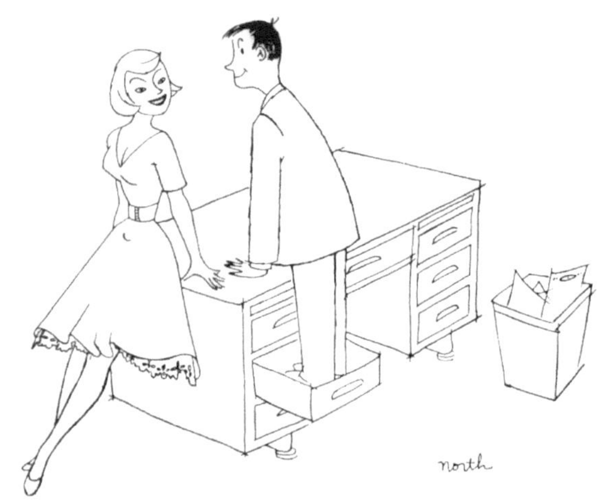

"You know Benny, I just adore tall men."

Business and Painting

After 10 years at MBL in Newark, I took a position in Manhattan with a public relations agency, and over the next several years moved up the corporate ladder through a variety of PR positions. After two years working as a consultant to the Cunard Line, they asked me to join the company as Vice President/Public Affairs in 1970. While at Cunard's headquarters in New York City, I continued to develop myself as a painter by studying at the Art Students' League and The New School.

When our three kids began leaving the nest, we sold our house in Edison, NJ, and moved south to Toms River at the Jersey shore. There, I continued to commute to my job in Manhattan, but spent as much time as I could painting in my small home studio, and also found time to paint outdoors. With enough completed art work to finally show and sell, my wife and I started a gallery and gift shop called *North's Wharf*. It was tucked inside a lobster and fish market, and run on weekdays by Colleen. Located near a fishing dock at the Manasquan Inlet, it provided the opportunity to paint commercial fishing boats and nautical scenes on weekends. The boat owners and crew who sailed into the docks observed me at work. They were tough but honest critics, and quick to point out errors I'd made in depicting the rigging or deck gear. Many asked me to paint portraits of their boats for them, and I was happy to oblige.

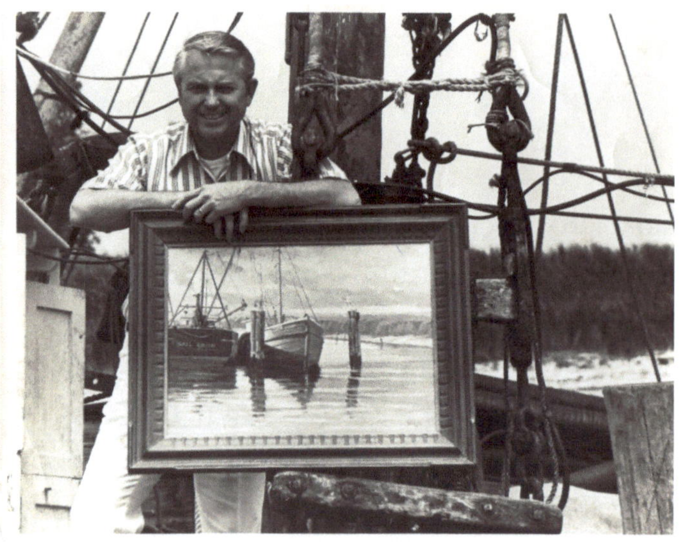
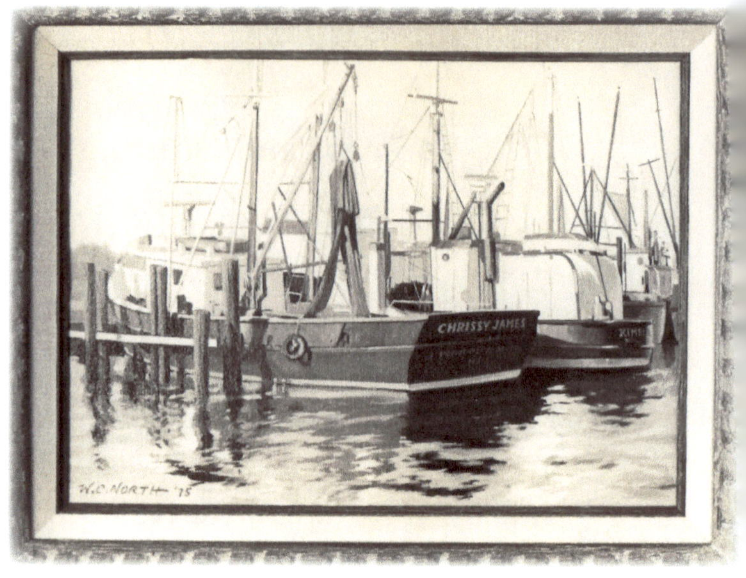

*The "Chrissy James" was probably the most meticulously maintained dragger in the
Manasquan fleet. This illustration was used as cover art for the invitation to Dad's one-
man show at Over the Rainbow Gallery in Point Pleasant Beach, New Jersey.
Sadly, the Chrissy James ended up on the beach after the clutch failed,
but the boat owner at least has the painting.*

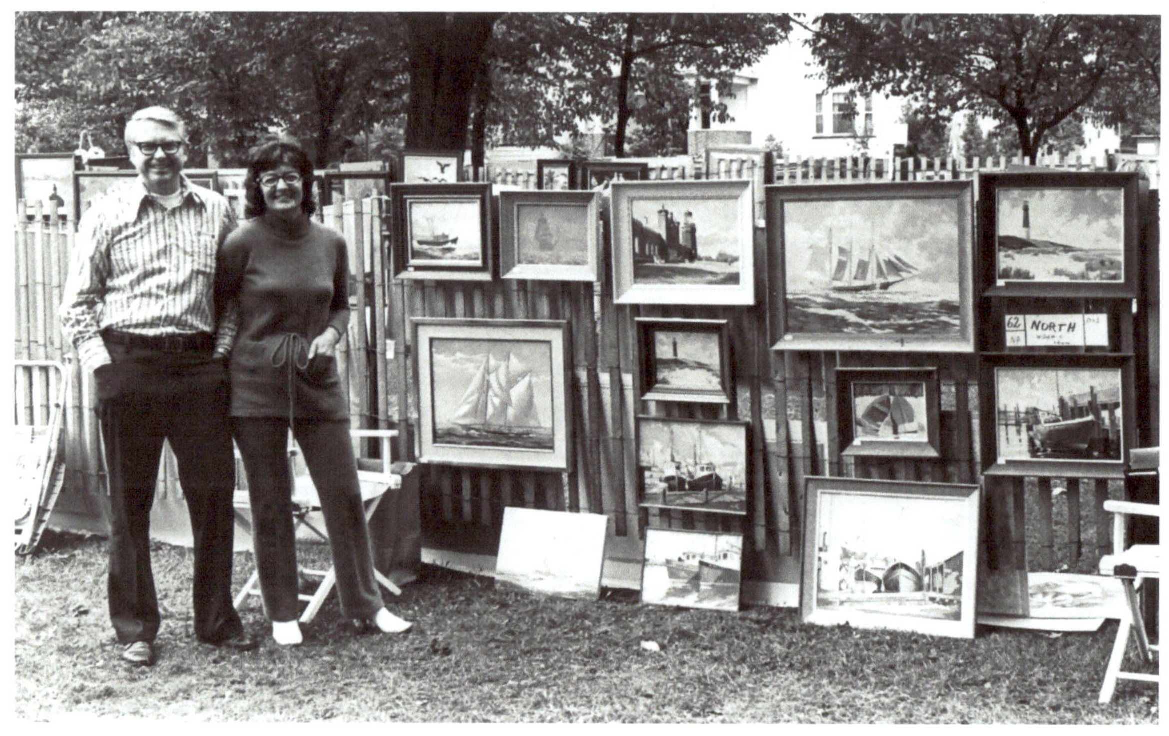

*Outdoor shows were weekend fun for Mom and Dad. Dad took third place
in the oil painting category in this 1971 Metuchen, New Jersey, exhibit.
Exhibited at the event were his popular dragger paintings and one of Barnegat
Lighthouse, a subject he painted many times while living in New Jersey.*

Steadily working every spare hour, at nights and on weekends, I continued to produce work for my own gallery and others at the shore. Once there was an adequate inventory of saleable art, my wife and I would head out to an art show or festival somewhere along the Jersey shore. In a happy but unfortunate turn of events, sales were so good that after two years, I was unable to produce enough paintings to keep up with demand; we ran out of painting inventory and decided to close the shop.

My years with the Cunard Line were an exciting period in which we promoted the company's fleet of cruise ships, old and new. My responsibilities included marketing the transatlantic and cruise programs of the QE2, (which I painted several times), and a variety of Cunard hotels and resorts in the Caribbean and United Kingdom. Using historic photographs, I also painted the Carpathia, the ship that rescued survivors of the Titanic. I was also in charge of the introduction of several new ships, including the Cunard Princess, christened by Princess Grace of Monaco, the former Hollywood star Grace Kelly.

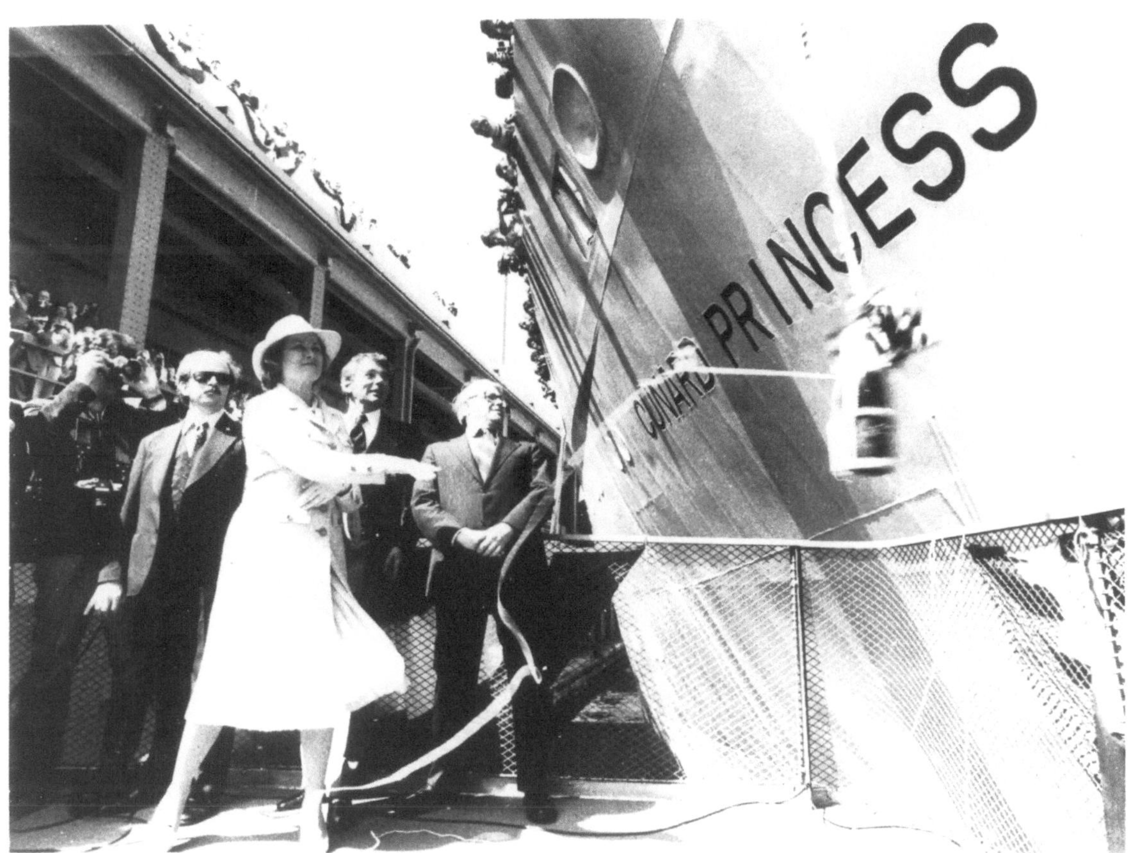

CUNARD PRINCESS   Naming Ceremony • March 30, 1977 • New York • by HSH Princess Grace of Monaco

Naming Ceremony,
March 30, 1977, in New York City by HSH Princess Grace of Monaco.

In 1978 I left Cunard after 10 years to become director of public relations for the Mystic Seaport Museum in Mystic, Connecticut. Since I had a wide knowledge of maritime and tourism industry matters, this position seemed custom made for winding down from work life in the city. We moved to a new home in Connecticut just 15 minutes from the office, and this allowed for more time painting in my home studio.

During my 12 years in Mystic, I continued to study painting in workshops led by noted artist Charles Movalli. At the Movalli workshops, held on location, students were required to finish an oil painting in three hours. In my home studio, I was accustomed to the freedom to take three weeks to finish one, if I wanted. Once, while painting at a dock in Rockport, Massachusetts, I was having trouble with the perspective of the boat in the scene. Each time I checked it, the boat had changed its position. Because of the three-hour time frame, I was frantically working in a loose and casual style, in the zone, toward finishing the painting in time. Eventually I realized that the boat's position was changing because the tide was falling. They say time and tide wait for no man, so I stopped both in my mind's eye and successfully completed the painting. That one piece of finished work brought me such great pleasure, we kept it in our private collection for many years. The passion I felt while creating it must have come through, because when it was finally offered, it sold fast in our Florida gallery.

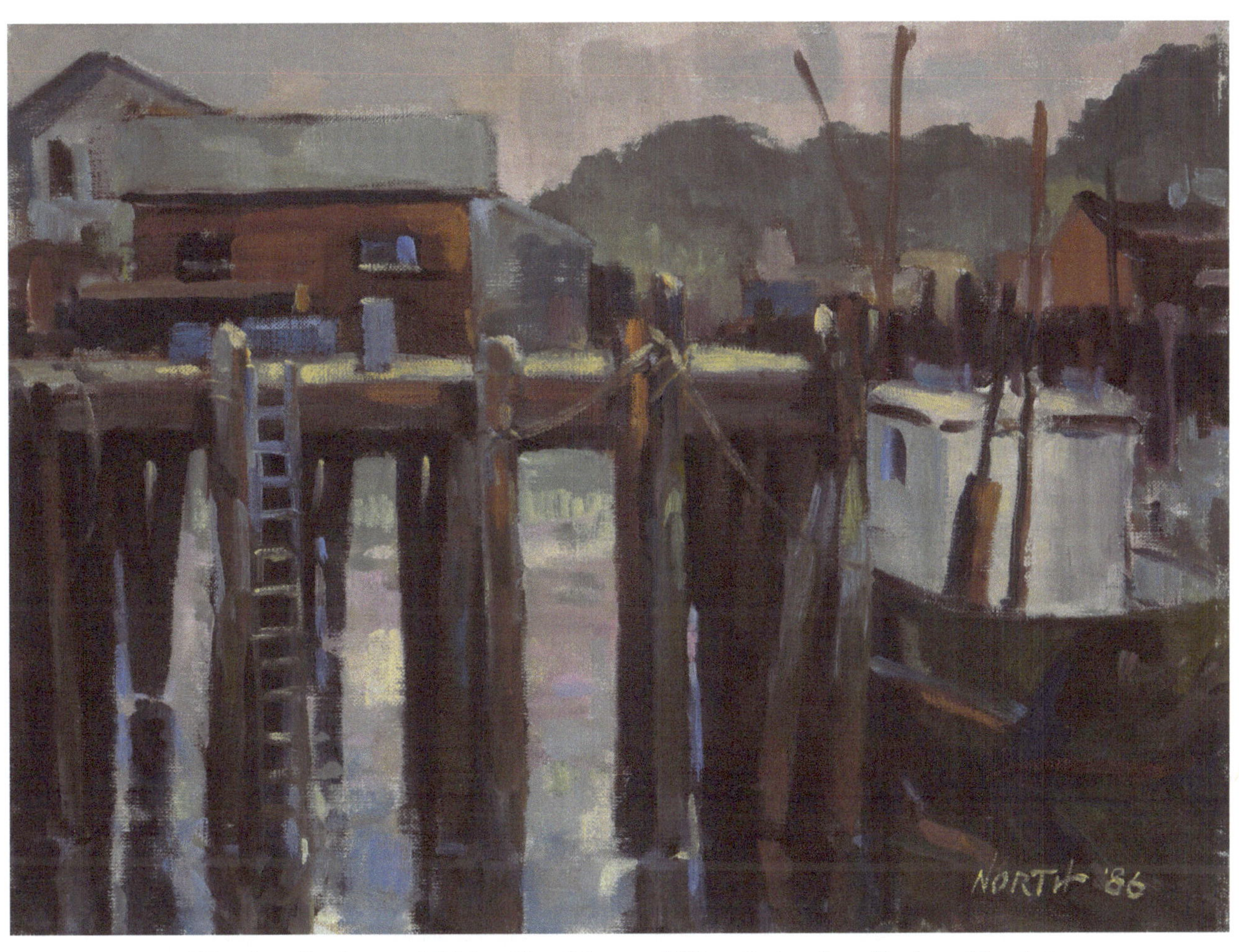

*"Dock at Rockport, MA"—The tide was falling faster than Dad could paint,
but that eventually taught him an important lesson
and the story had a happy ending when he realized what was happening.*

In Connecticut, I also had more time to be involved with art organizations, and became an elected artist member of the Lyme Art Association and the Mystic Art Association. Now that I was not commuting long hours to work, I also had time to undertake a concentrated period of study at night and on weekends at the Lyme Academy of Fine Art, under the tutelage of Deanne Keller, Dan Gheno and Jerry Caron. During these years my work was shown in area galleries in Connecticut and Rhode Island, and was selling rather well. My art subjects during this time in my life were reflective of my Mystic Seaport Museum experience, and my themes were ships at Mystic Seaport and the local New England landscape.

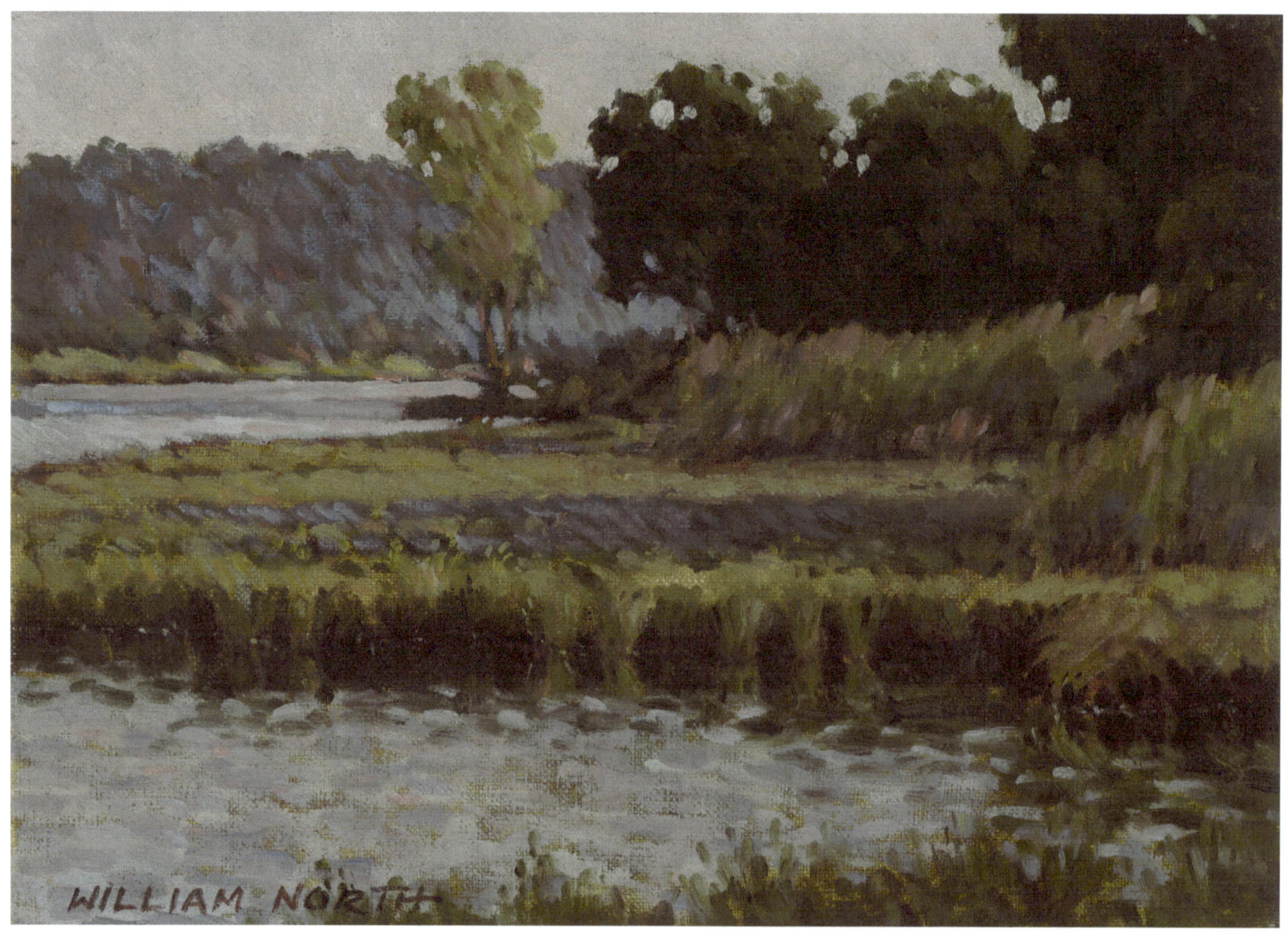

Mystic River Shoreline

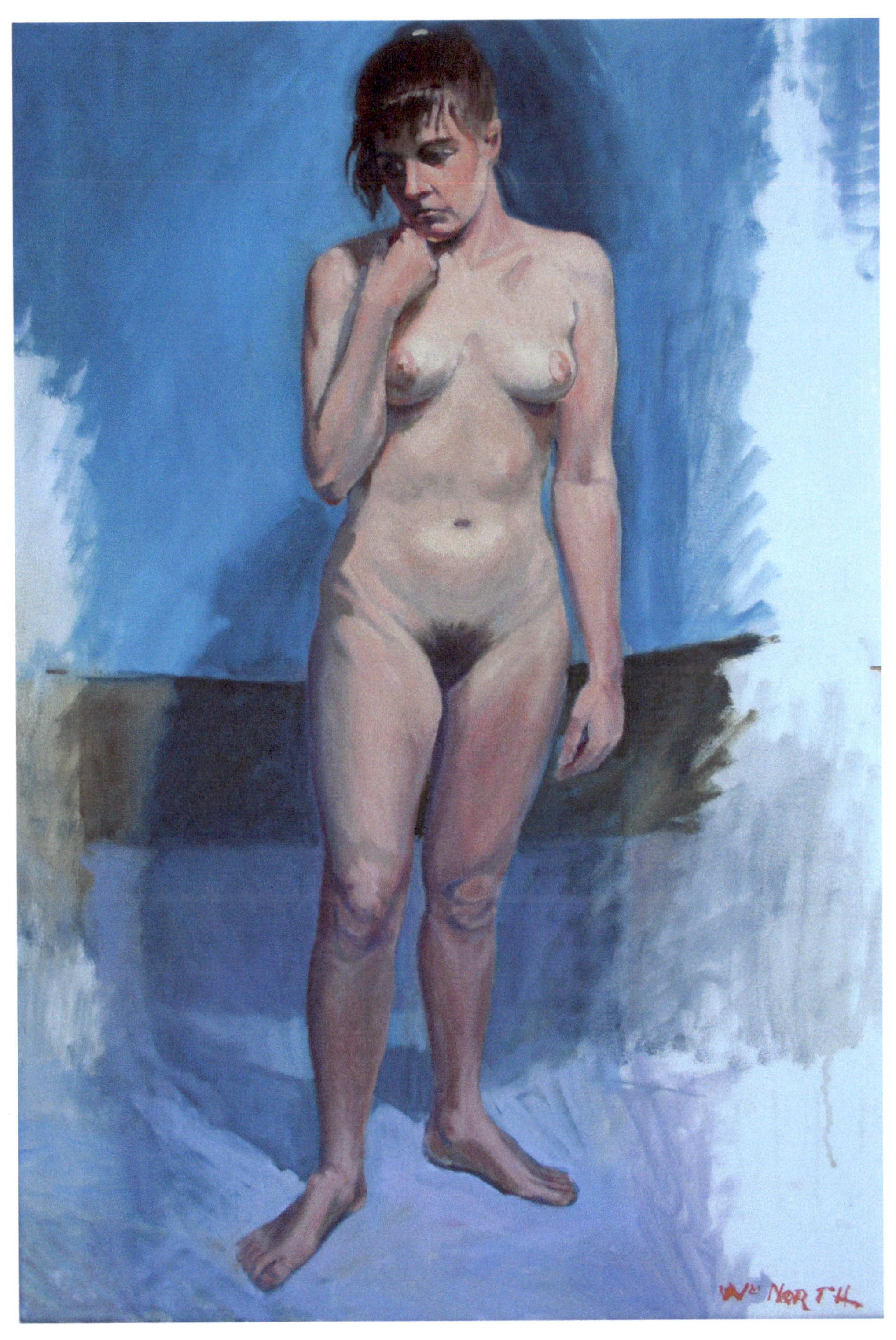

Figure painting: "Jennifer" Oil on Canvas, 24" x 48"

In 1987 I took a two-week trip to American Samoa to visit my daughter, Debby, who had moved there to work for an auto importer. There I started 14 paintings in 14 days, shipped them home, and finished them all in my studio. These included *Rainmaker Mountain* and *Pago Pago Harbor*. My technique was still taking shape.

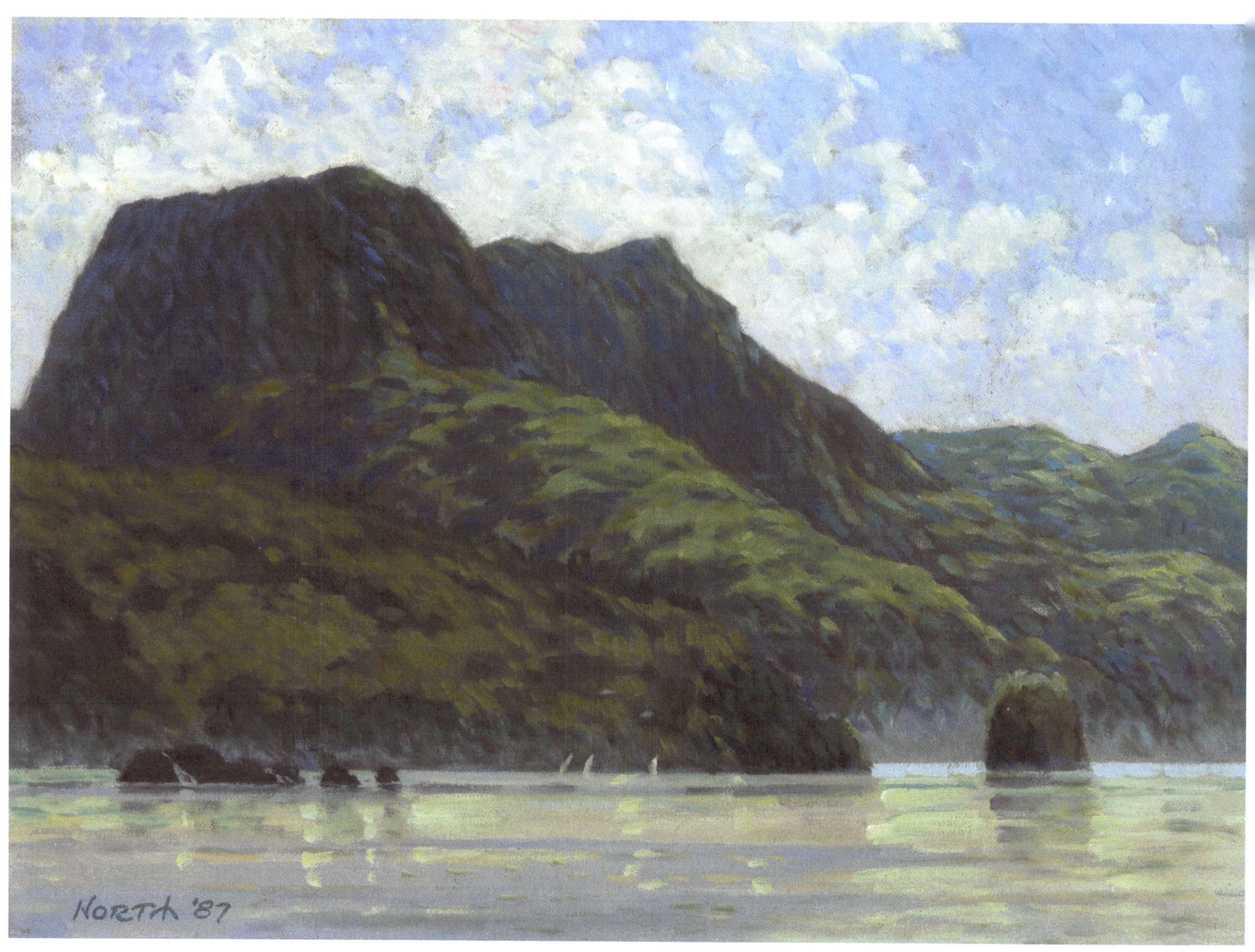

Rainmaker Mountain with Flower Pot Rock, American Samoa.

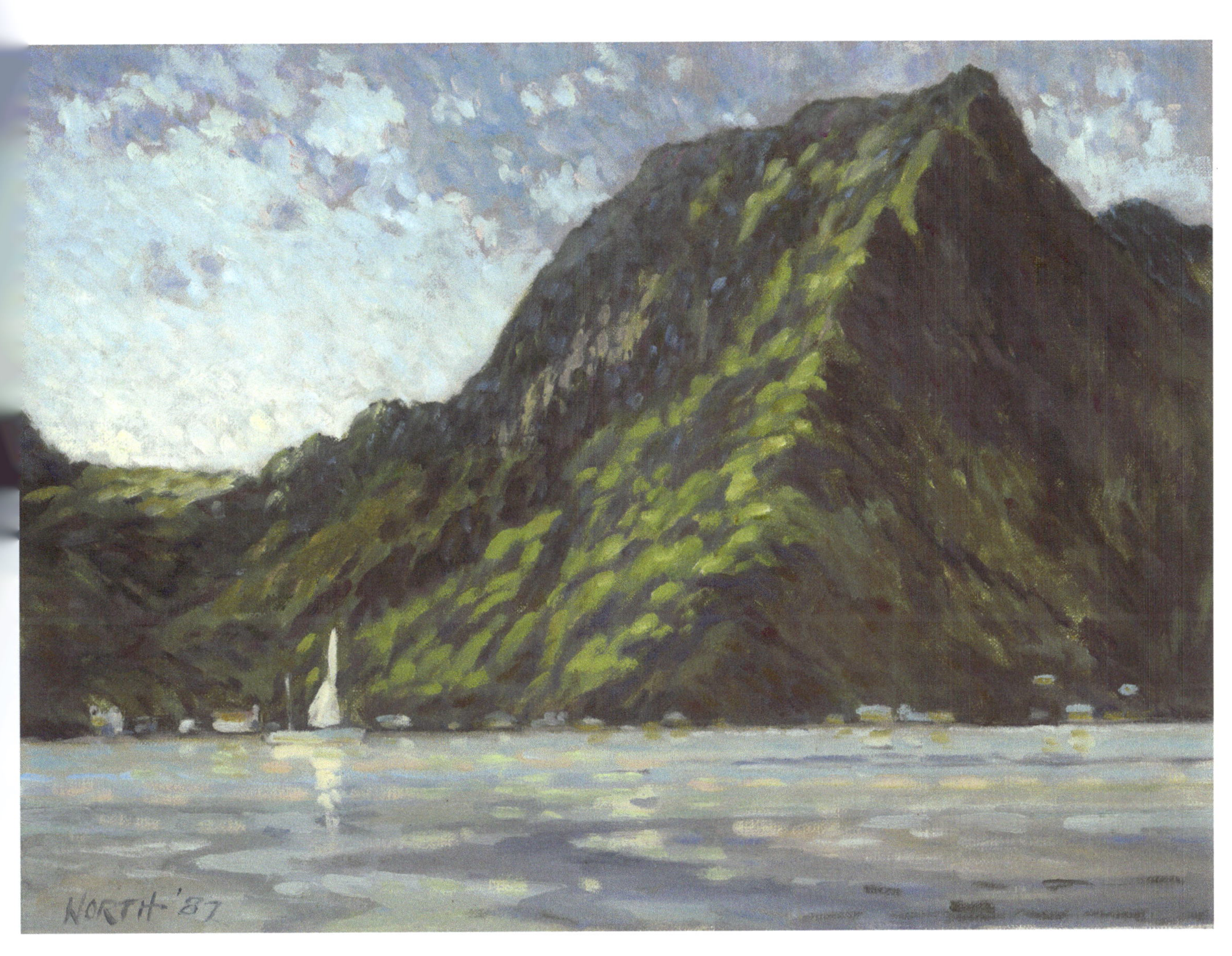

Matefeo Mountain on the other side of Pago Pago Harbor.

It was in the misty mornings and brilliant fall foliage of Connecticut that my style took on the impressionistic look it still has today. According to tradition, I carried my painting supplies outdoors to work en plein aire, and created the habit of painting landscapes outdoors from life. Still lifes, of mostly florals and sea shells, were painted in my Connecticut studio.

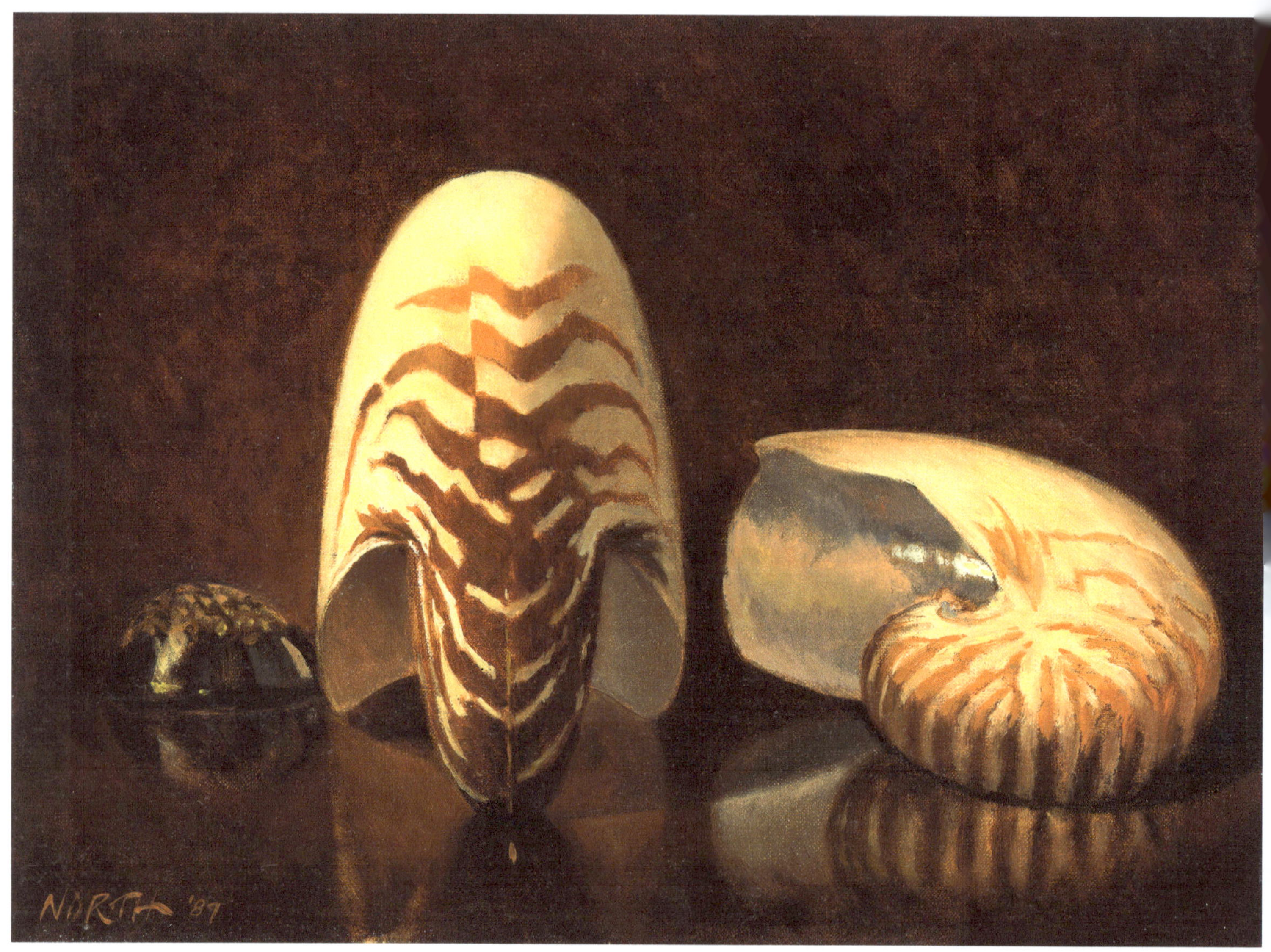

Nautilus & Cowrie, Connecticut Studio, May 1986, 12" x 16"

The Sunshine State

Those twelve years of experience gained in workshops and through many hours at the easel, fed my confidence in my artistic abilities, until I felt ready to consider devoting full time to a painting career. Finally, in 1990, at age 62, I opted for early retirement from the business world. Colleen and I left New England for southern Florida where the climate would allow me to paint year-round and where there were so many beautiful painting locations. For several weeks we drove up and down Florida's West Coast, exploring one town after another, and eventually settled in Fort Myers. Fort Myers was close to diverse landscapes, like Sanibel Island and Captiva Island, many state and local parks, and to The Everglades. It's also located midway between two culturally rich cities with numerous art galleries: Sarasota and Naples.

Painting and Teaching

In those early Florida years, I plunged into painting with an unfettered abandon. It had taken me so many years to be able to say I was a full-time artist, and I wanted to make the most of every single day. I soon became a member of the San Cap Art League and the Fort Myers Beach Art Association, two of the most active artist groups in the area. Once I began to paint the local landscape, I produced scenes of mangroves, palm hammocks and Florida pasture. I'd head out every morning with my painting supplies, and plenty of sunscreen and bug spray, and paint until the heat became unbearable. I was learning to see a landscape that was new to me, and happily accepted the challenge to immerse myself in the process.

As I became known as a local artist, I found there was a demand for art instruction in oil painting in the traditional style, which was my specialty. So when asked by some of the local organizations to teach, I didn't say no. I taught oil painting in Sanibel, Naples, Bonita Springs and Fort Myers over a period of five years, retiring four separate times because the demands of teaching simply took too much time away from my own painting. By then I was entering paintings in shows, so I eventually needed to give up the instruction altogether and just paint. It was what I had yearned after for so long, after all.

In 1995, I was thrilled to be a first place prize winner in the well-regarded regionally important Winner's Circle Competition and fortunate over the years to win numerous awards and money prizes in several others.

With my reputation expanding, in 2004 I was invited to display 24 paintings in The Department of State's Governor's Gallery located in the entryway to the Governor's office in Tallahassee. I was honored to hold the distinction of being the first Lee County artist to be invited to show there.

Beaches

Paintings of Florida beaches became an important part of my repertoire, and I painted many beach scenes in the first four years we lived in the Sunshine State. But it was the beach at Delnor-Wiggins Pass State Park, which I discovered in 1994, that became my personal painter's paradise. The shadow patterns there are a constant source of inspiration, lasting from sunrise until late morning — the perfect time to paint outdoors. The impression of the early morning shadows cast on the sand by the Australian Pines and palm trees captivated my artist's eye. For the next ten years I painted there almost every day, and in February 2007 I had the honor to be named the Park's first Artist in Residence.

The Florida Department of Environmental Protection's announcement of the distinction noted, "The artist was selected on the basis of the quality and appropriateness of his work and his long history of painting in the Park." Painting on location at the park was made even more enjoyable by the staff, which treated me like royalty. Although I no longer paint outdoors there, the many friends I've made stay in touch.

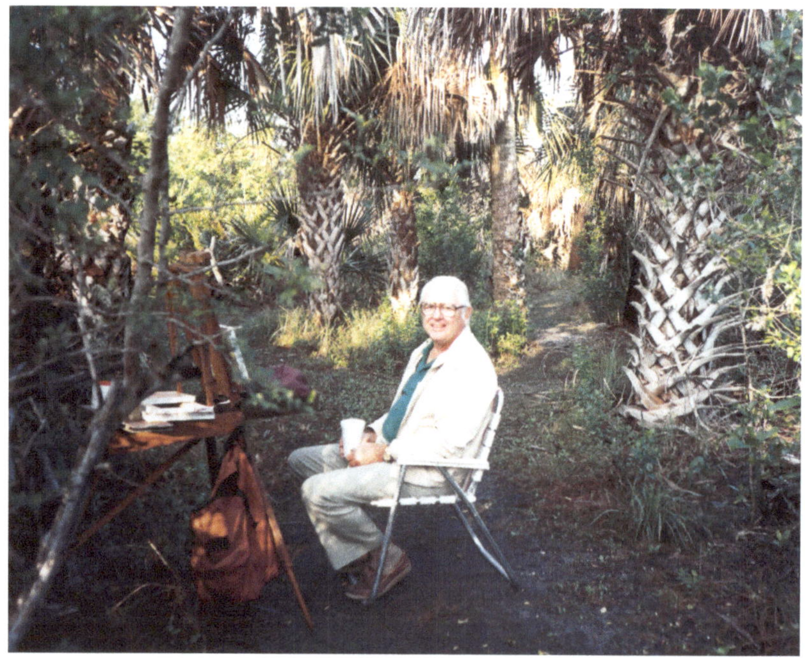

The setting is beautiful to the artist's eye, but getting to this spot in Sanibel's Nature Conservancy was difficult. The reward was the dense Florida foliage and a unique subject to paint. Dad sometimes shared the location with a passing alligator or snake, and often with the resident no-see-ums.

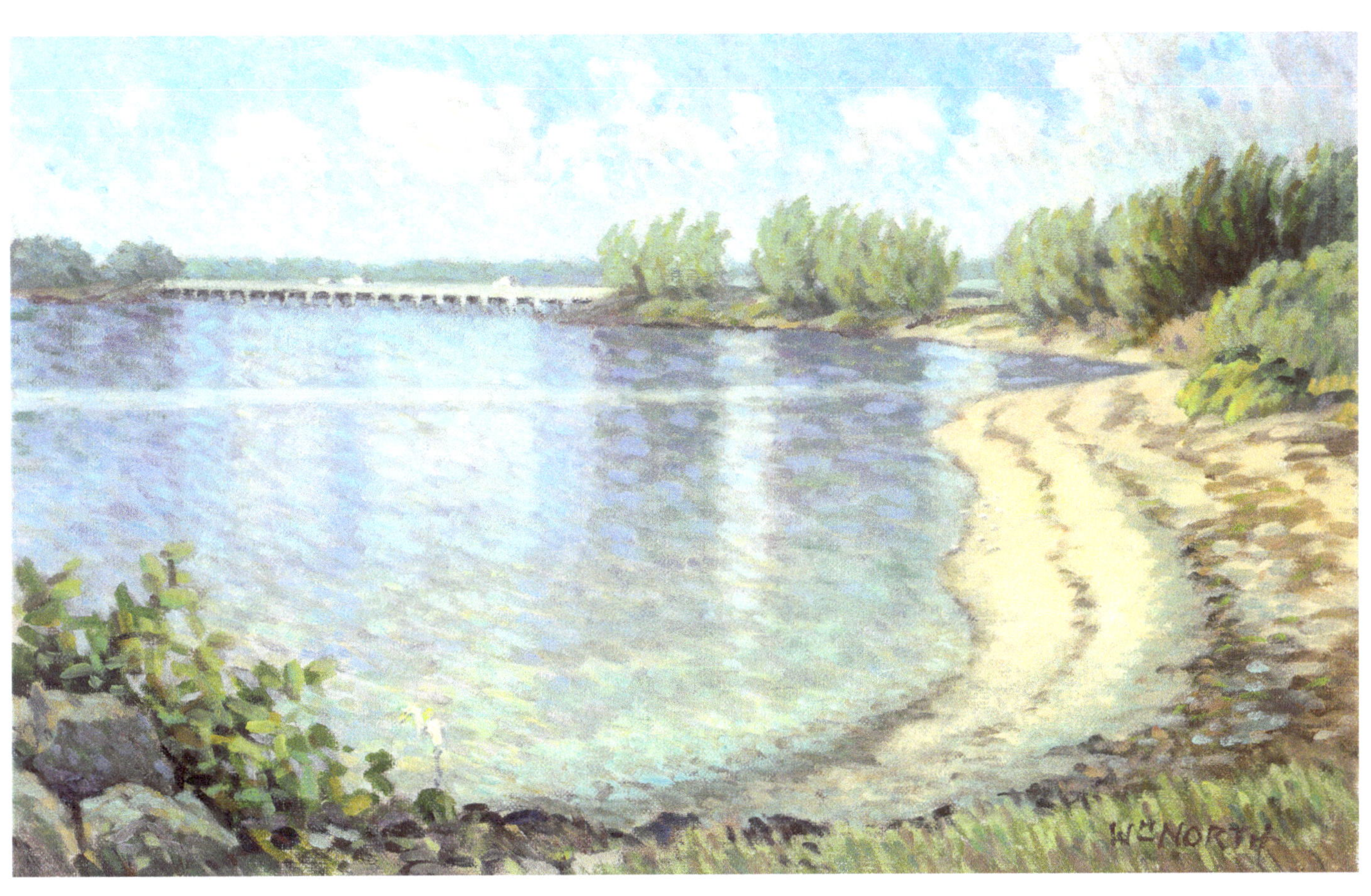

Sanibel Causeway, Florida

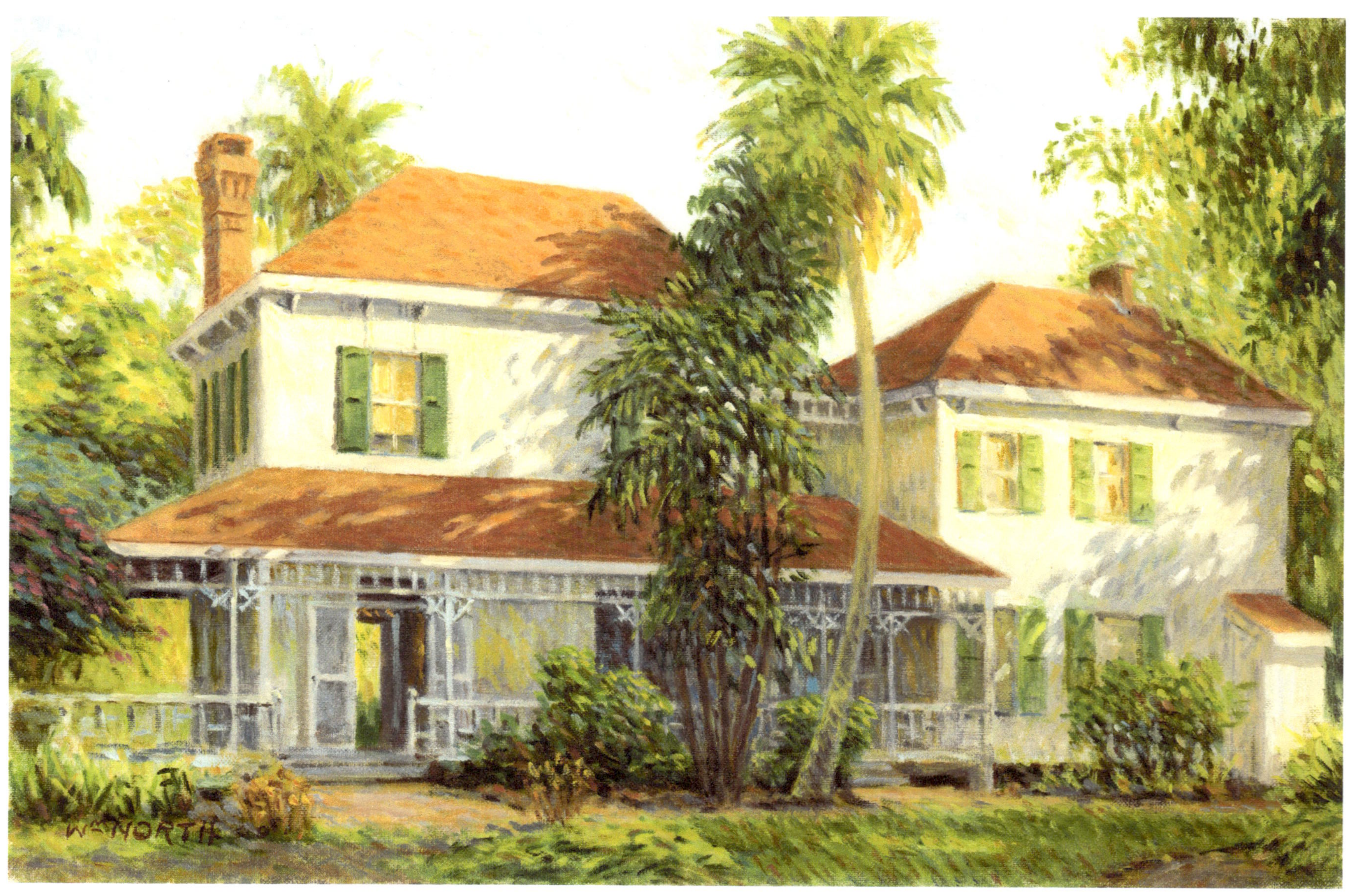

Thomas Edison Winter Home, Edison Museum, Fort Myers, Florida

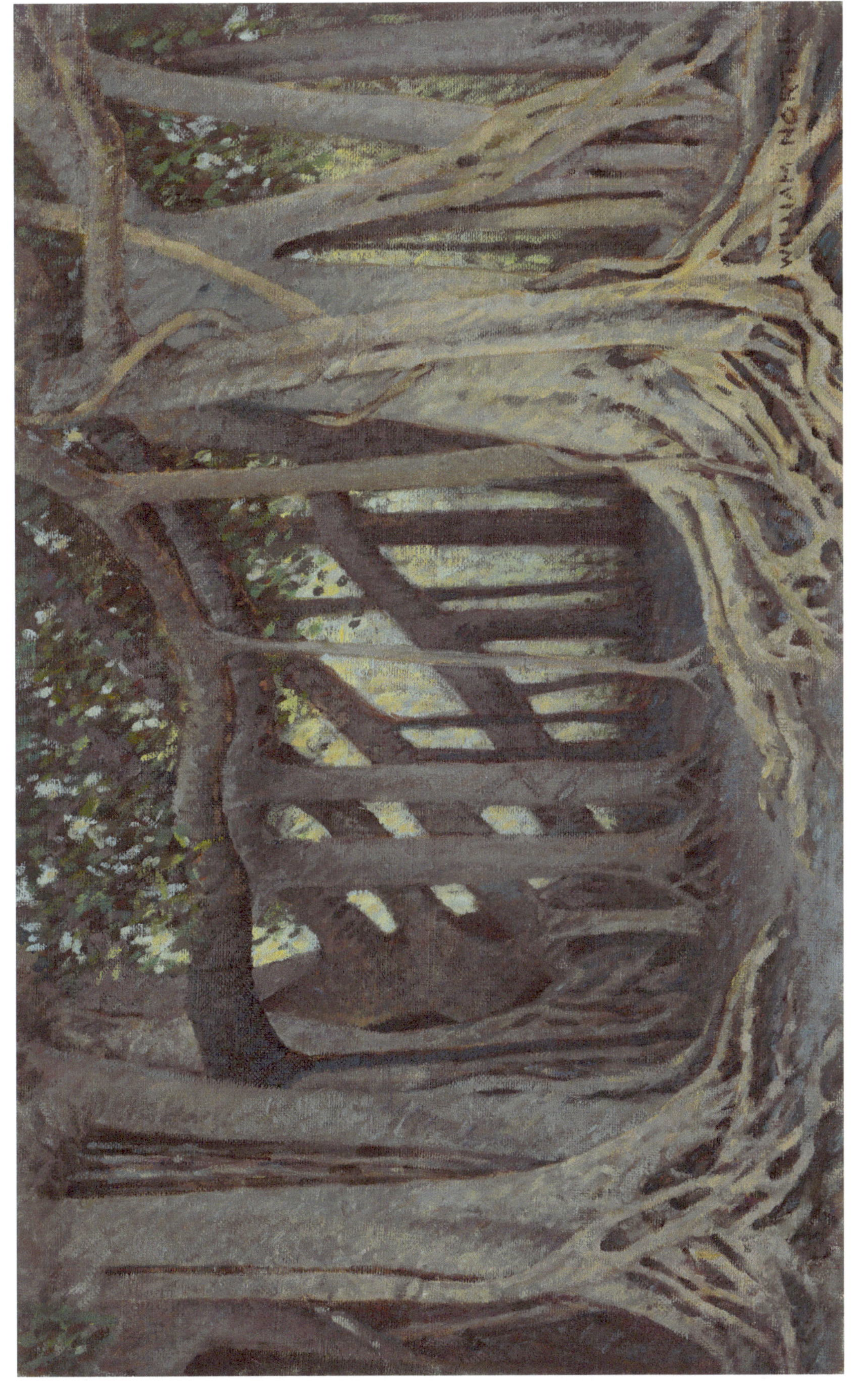

Thomas Edison Banyan Tree, Edison Museum Grounds, Fort Myers, Florida

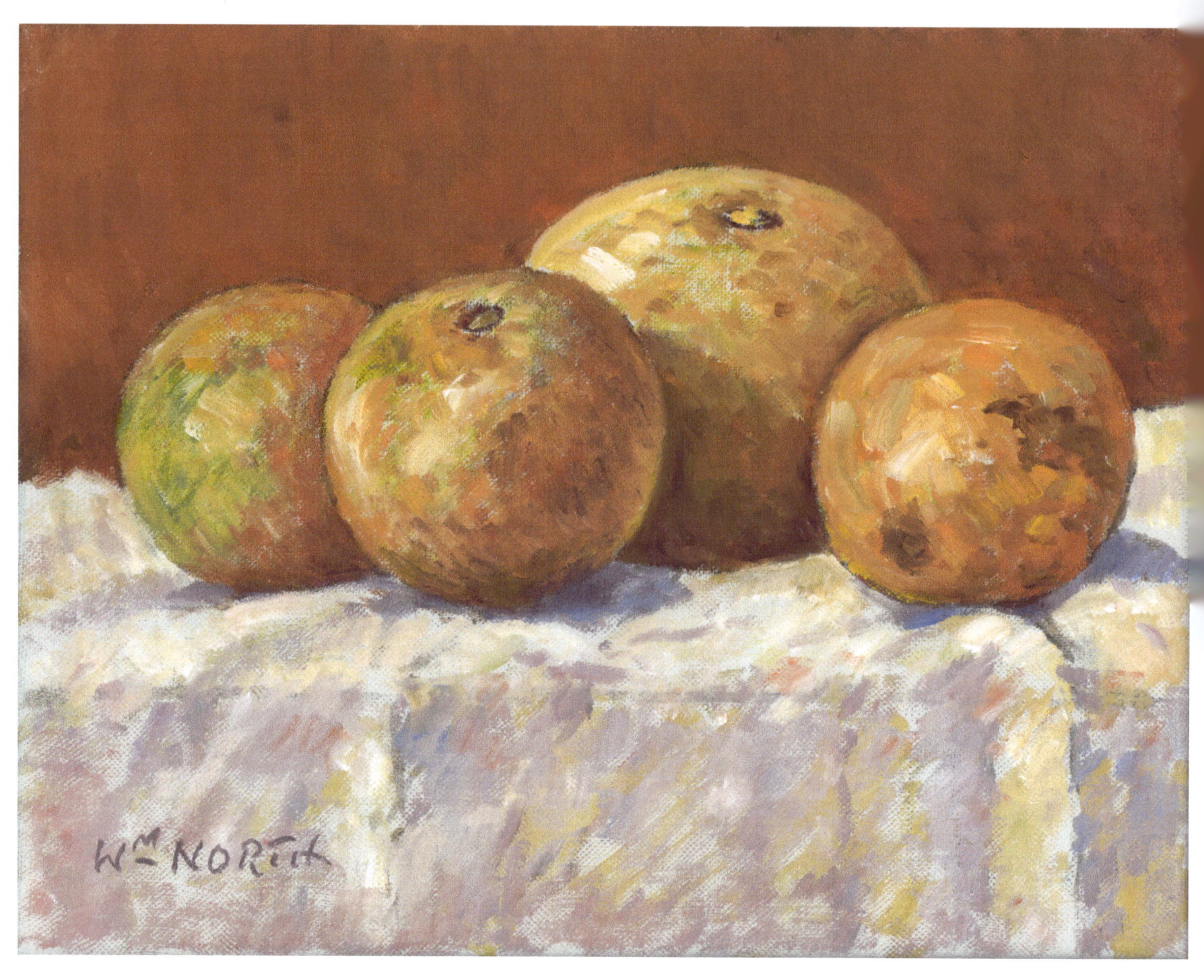

Rhode Reds and Ruby Red

Oranges

Around 1995 so much of my work was tied up in local Southwest Florida galleries that I no longer needed to enter competitions. I was now selling enough of my original oil paintings to require a rigorous painting schedule to keep the galleries supplied. I was elated when this rewarding set of circumstances I'd imagined for so many years was finally coming true. As a complement to my outdoor landscapes, I went looking for an indoor painting theme that I could work on in the studio in the afternoons.

One day, Colleen and I happened to stop by a local produce stand, where I saw the brilliant piles of Florida juice oranges. We bought a bagful, took them home and I arranged them in a traditional still life scene. That's how my now-popular Florida citrus theme paintings began, and I still add new paintings to my *Real Florida Oranges* series every year.

As a subject, the Florida orange provides endless possibilities. Its shape is not perfectly round, and its coloring not perfectly orange, as popular images would have us think. Instead, the orange's colors range from yellow to brown to green to red, to orange. Some fruit have dark markings on their skins called 'wind scars' caused by a twig or leaf brushing against the orange as it grows on the tree.

As an artist, I find endless beauty in all this variety, and carefully select each individual orange for its unique character. With such diversity in the fruit, every painting really is a portrait of individuals—individual oranges.

As I painted the oranges in still life, my interest in citrus increased, and I began to visit local orange groves and soon realized the possibilities of portraying the groves in landscapes, and thus another new theme was born.

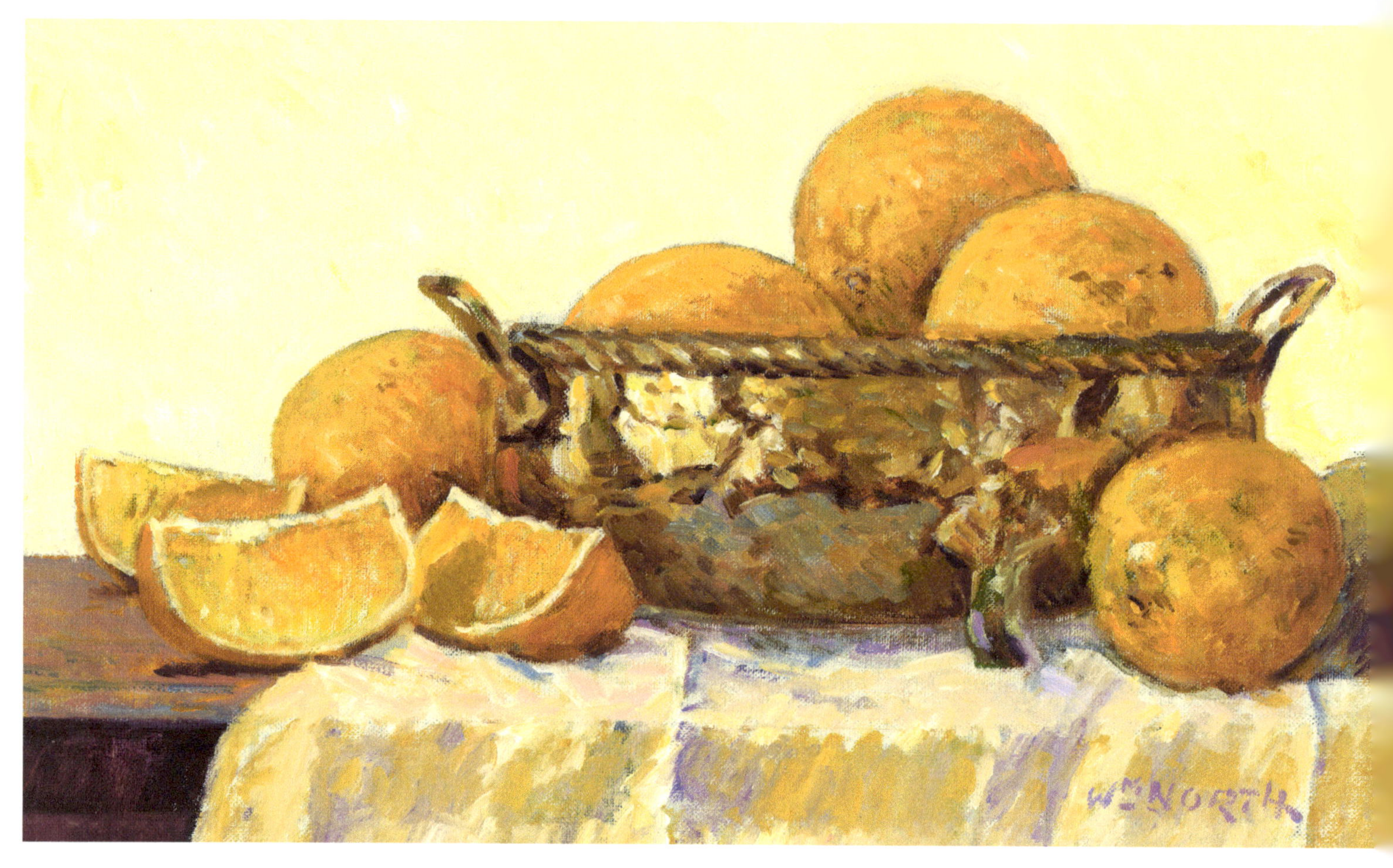

Red Valencias from Florida

While living, painting and selling art in the Sunshine State, my paintings of oranges have been noticed by Florida growers. Over the years I developed a special relationship with the Gulf Citrus Growers Association which purchased many of my original paintings to present to citrus industry honorees. Individual members of the association, and others in the industry, have also purchased my paintings for their personal enjoyment. Years ago I was invited to show my oils at the annual Citrus Expo, amid John Deere tractors, citrus harvesting machines and irrigation systems.

At one show in particular, I was approached by a grapefruit grower who asked why I didn't paint grapefruit. I had no real answer, so I told him I would, and I did. In this citrus industry environment, grove owners compliment me for painting oranges (and now grapefruit) as they really appear in nature, and some have purchased my paintings for their homes and offices, and to give as awards and gifts.

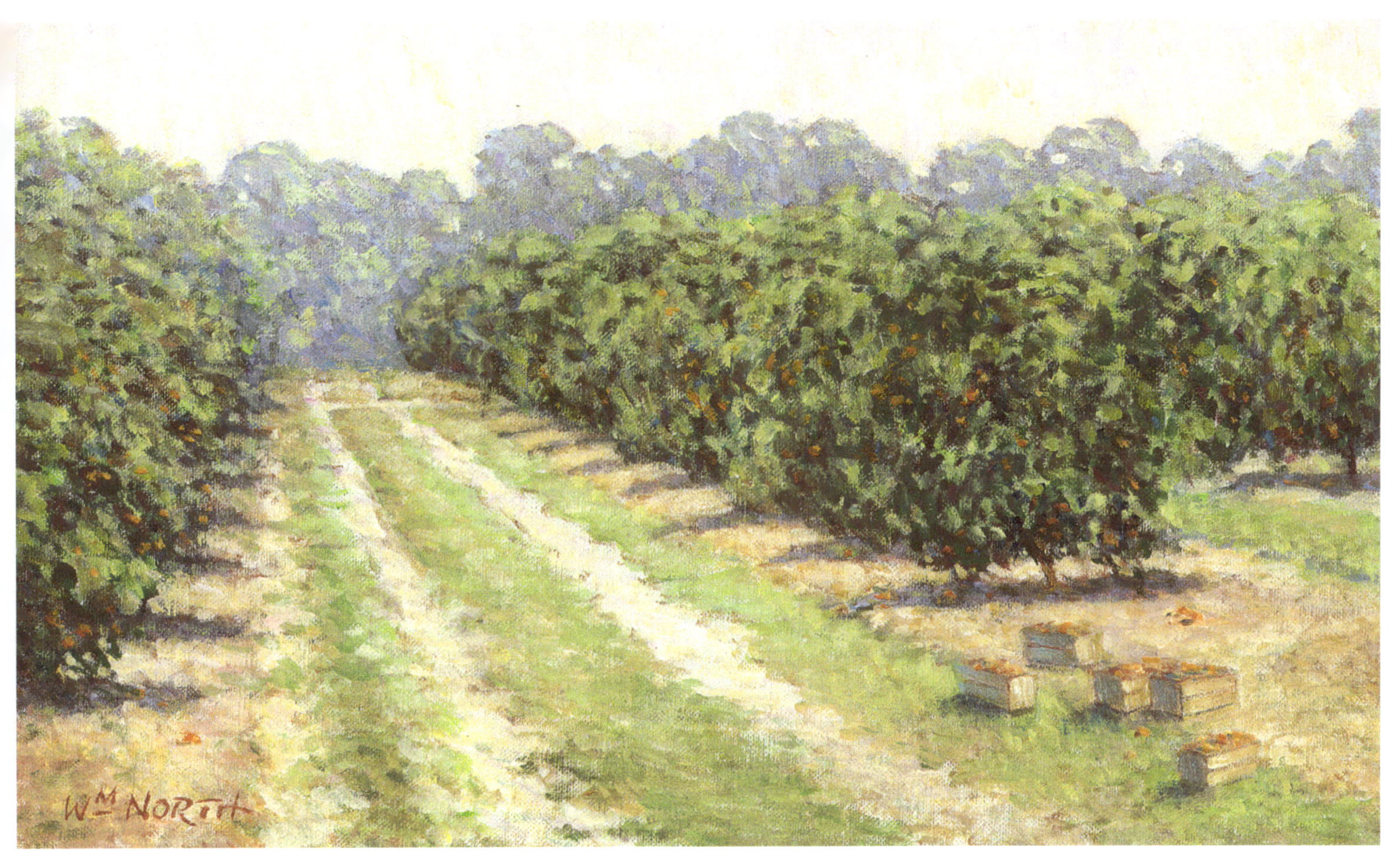

Florida Orange Grove with Boxes

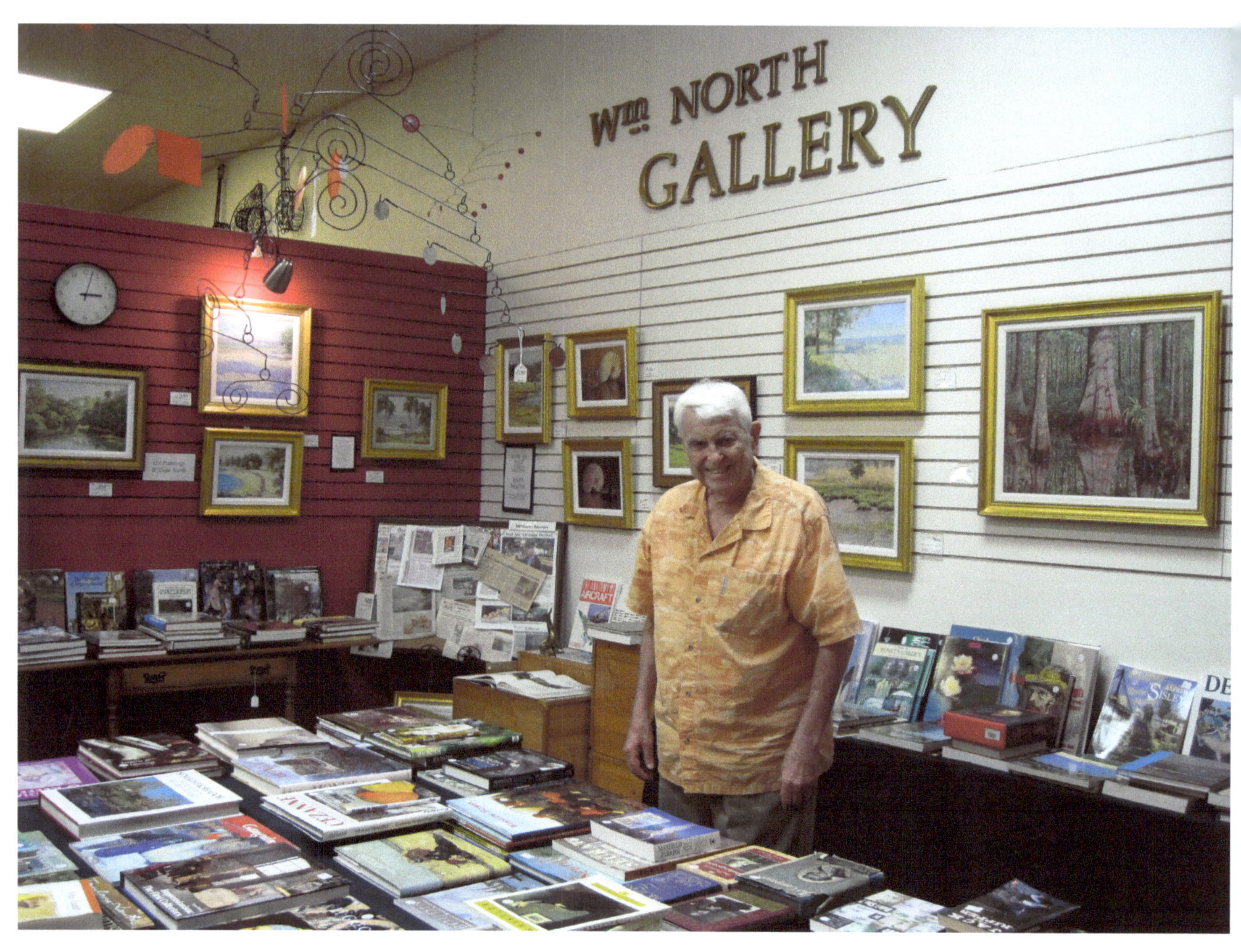

Dad in the Wm. North Gallery.

The Gallery

In 2004, well-known Florida architect and photographer Bruce Gora, and Gulf Coast University Professor Carl Schwartz and I founded the *Florida Fine Art Gallery* at Gannon's Antiques & Art Mall in South Fort Myers. For several years we forged an artist bond around the making and the business of art. In addition to our own work, we exhibited the work of many guest artists, and for a time the work of master potter and clay artist Ludmila Evans. She ultimately expanded into her own space in Gannon's Mall, and Bruce and Carl left to pursue other interests. Eventually the gallery became my baby.

The *Wm. North Gallery* now shows my paintings exclusively, plus the mobiles of noted metal sculptor Ralph Bigletti. We've expanded the space by adding a print gallery, offering reproductions of many of my paintings which were put into print beginning in 1995. More recently we've added a well-stocked *Art Book Store* with many unique and rare publications.

I think Degas got it right when he said good painting consists of variety with unity. He could have said the same about a good life. Throughout my life there were a great variety of interesting and exciting experiences unified by the common thread of a lifetime love of fine art. The opportunities to draw and paint and to achieve a dream come true—a career as a full-time professional painter—has been my crowning glory, for which I'm deeply grateful.

William North

Gallery

A Portfolio of Paintings
Past and Present

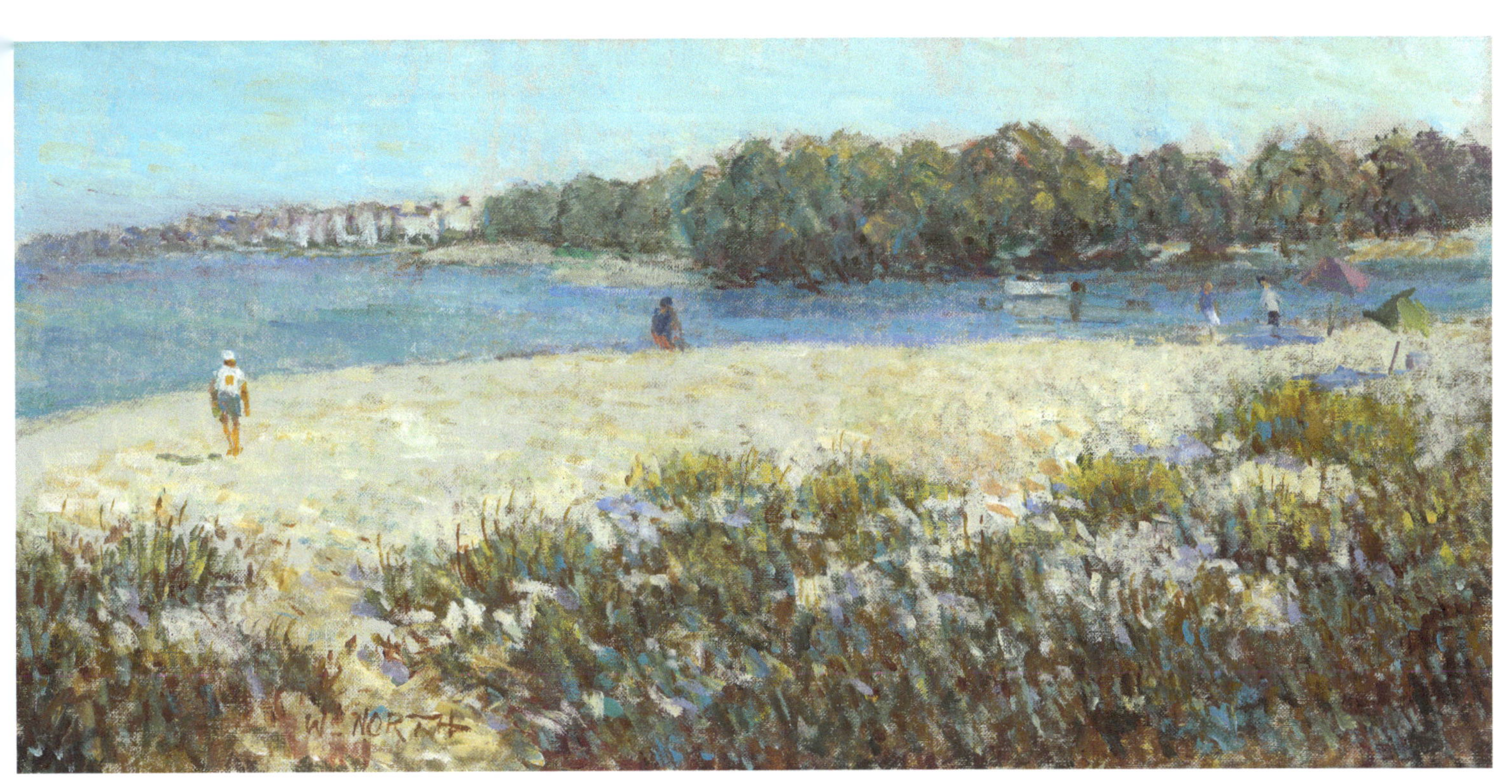

High Noon at Wiggins Pass, Naples, Florida

All Paintings are Oil on Linen Canvas

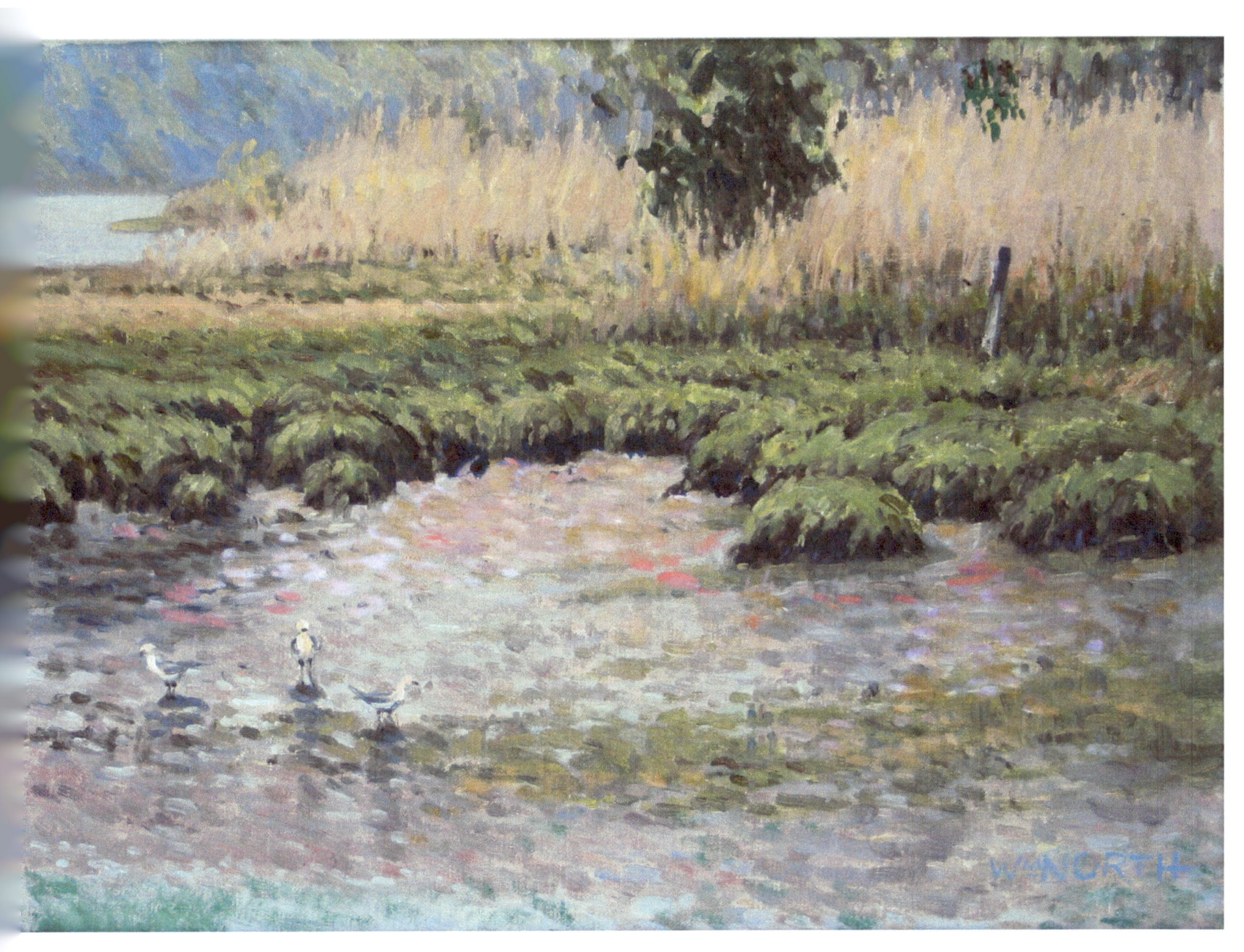

Headwaters of the Pequotsepos, Stonington, Connecticut, 1986, 11" x 14"

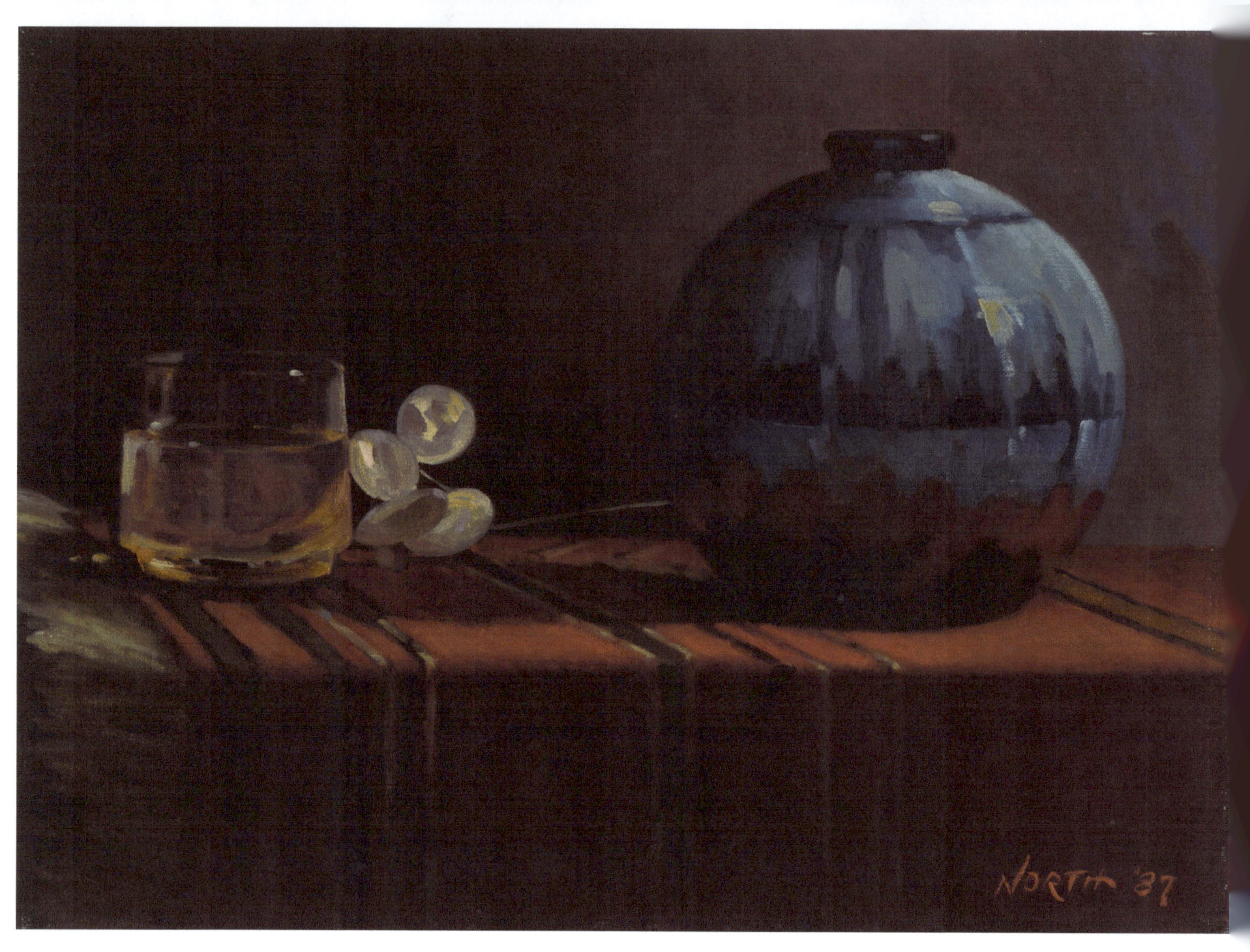

Blue Pot with Chinese Paper Money, Connecticut Studio, 1987, 12" x 16"

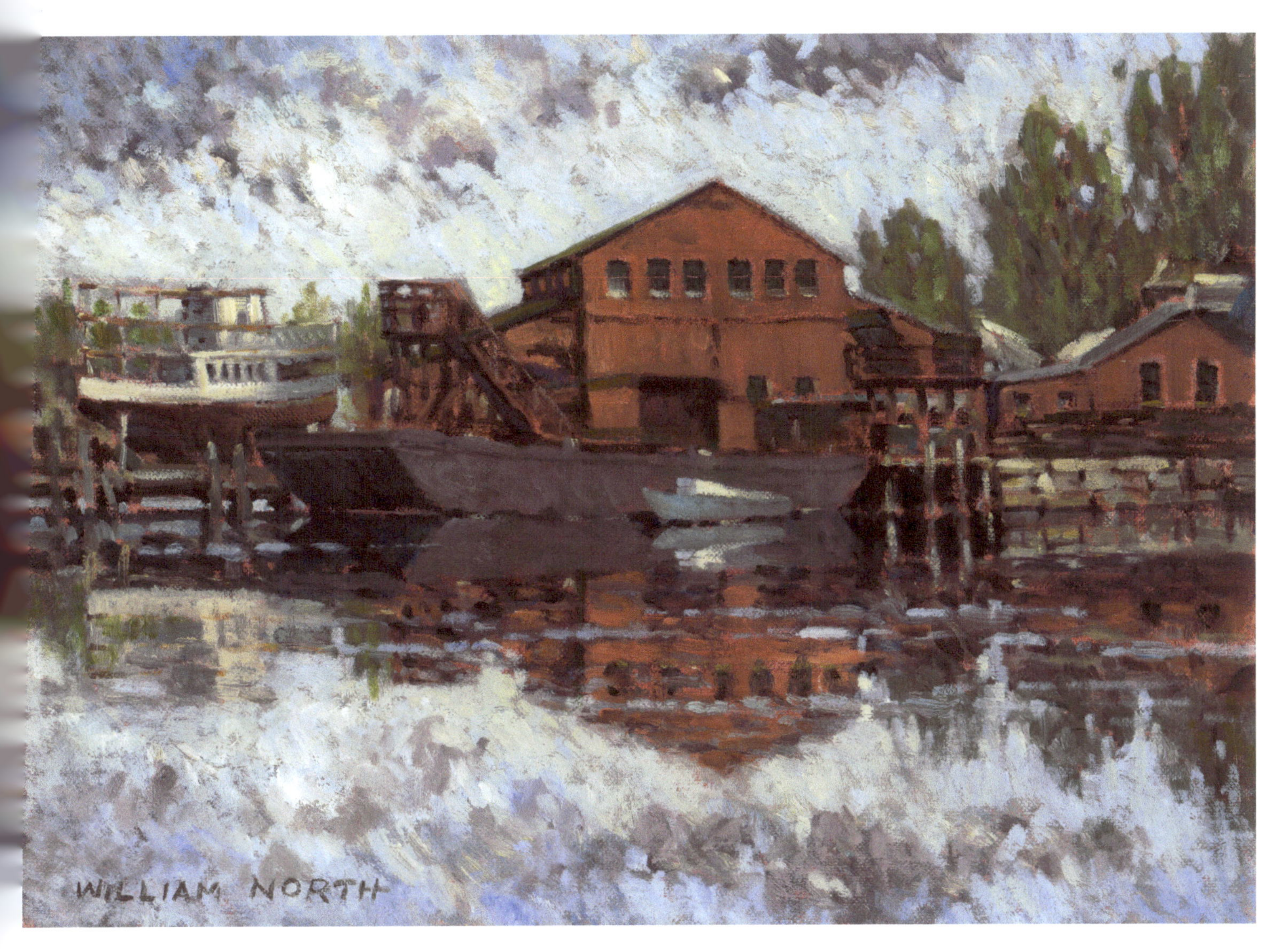

Mystic Seaport Restoration Shipyard, Connecticut, 9" x 12"

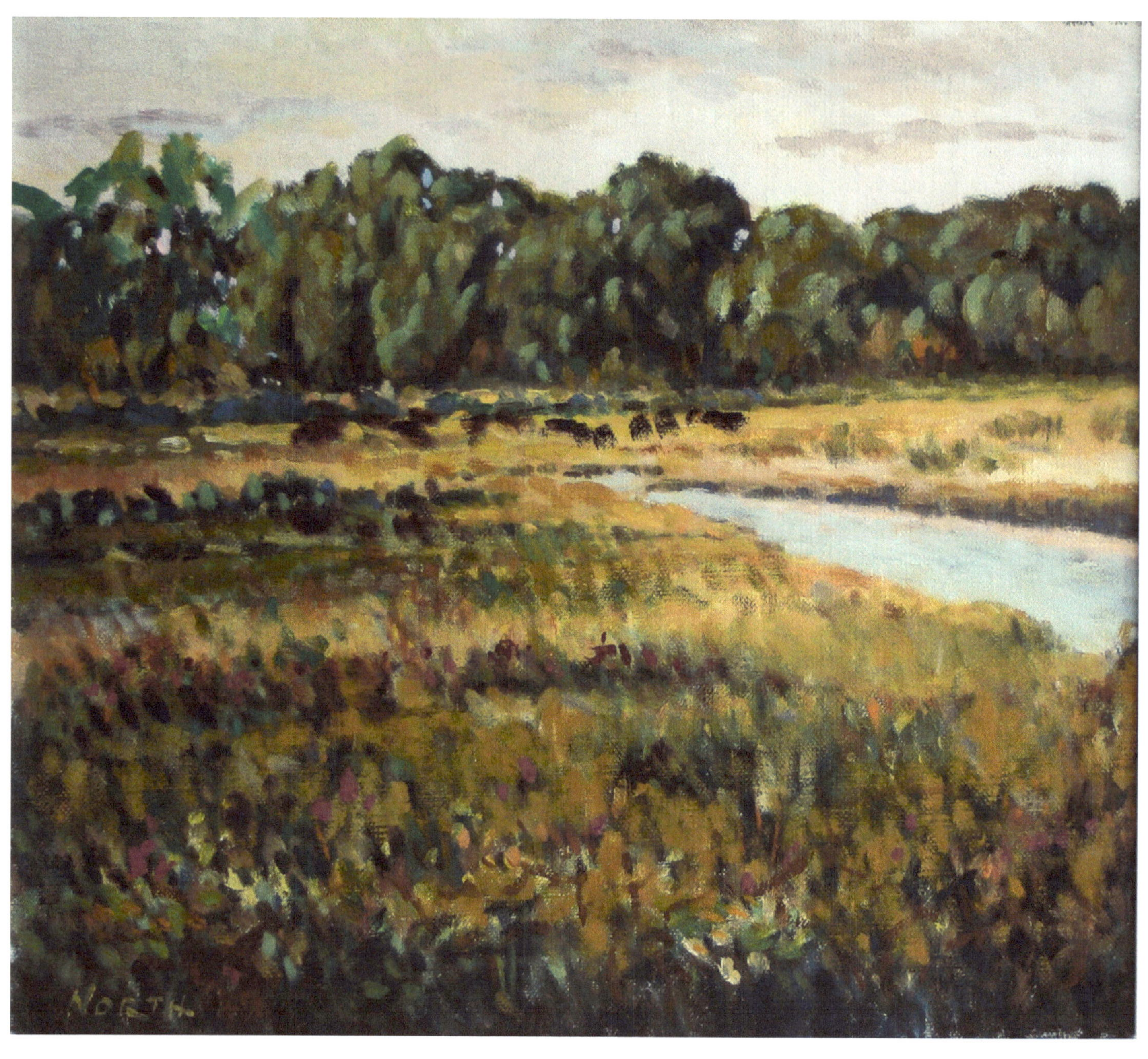

Barn Island Meadow, Connecticut, Jan. 1989, 9" x 12"

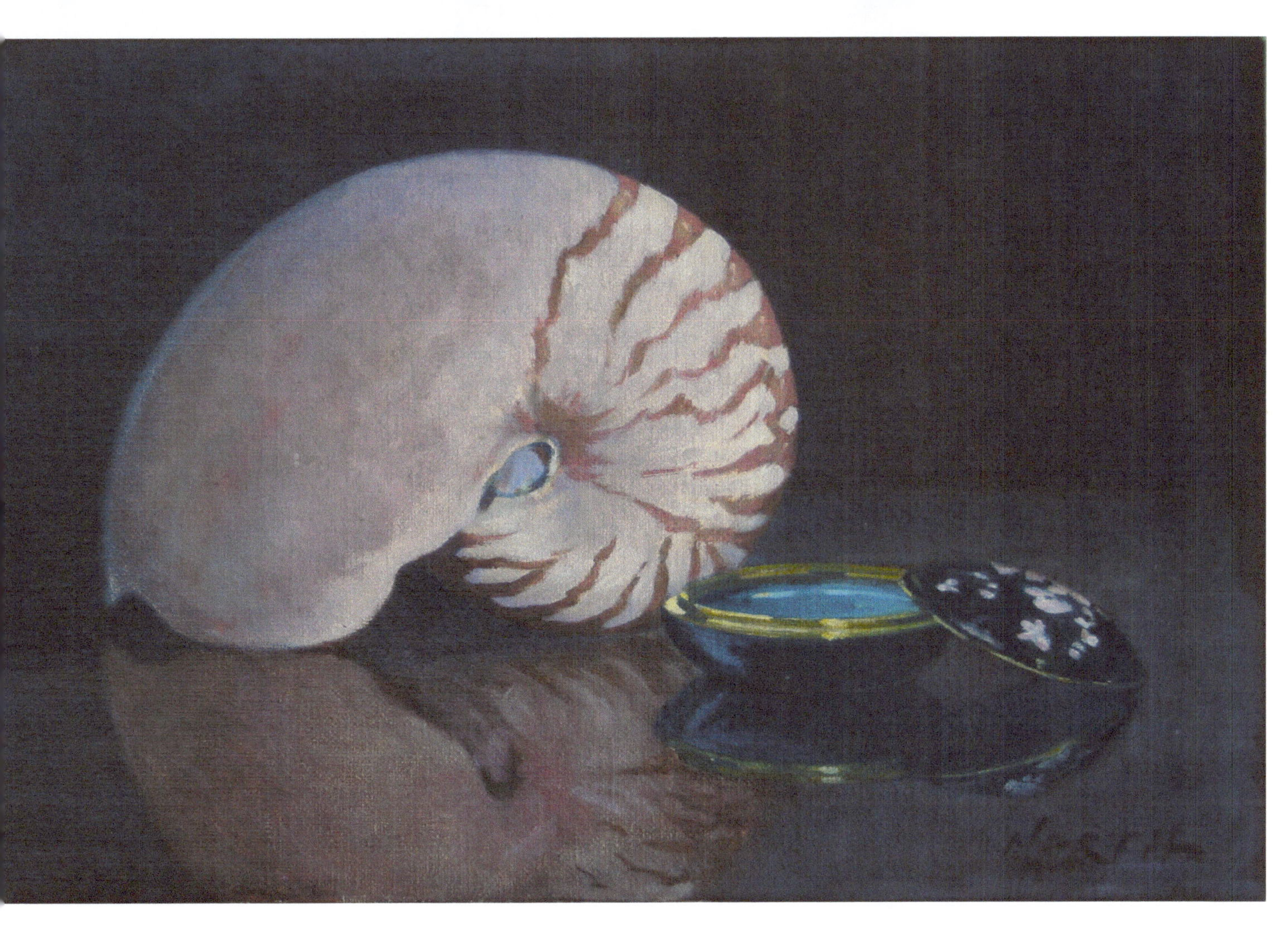

Nautilus with Enamel Box, Connecticut Studio, 9" x 12"

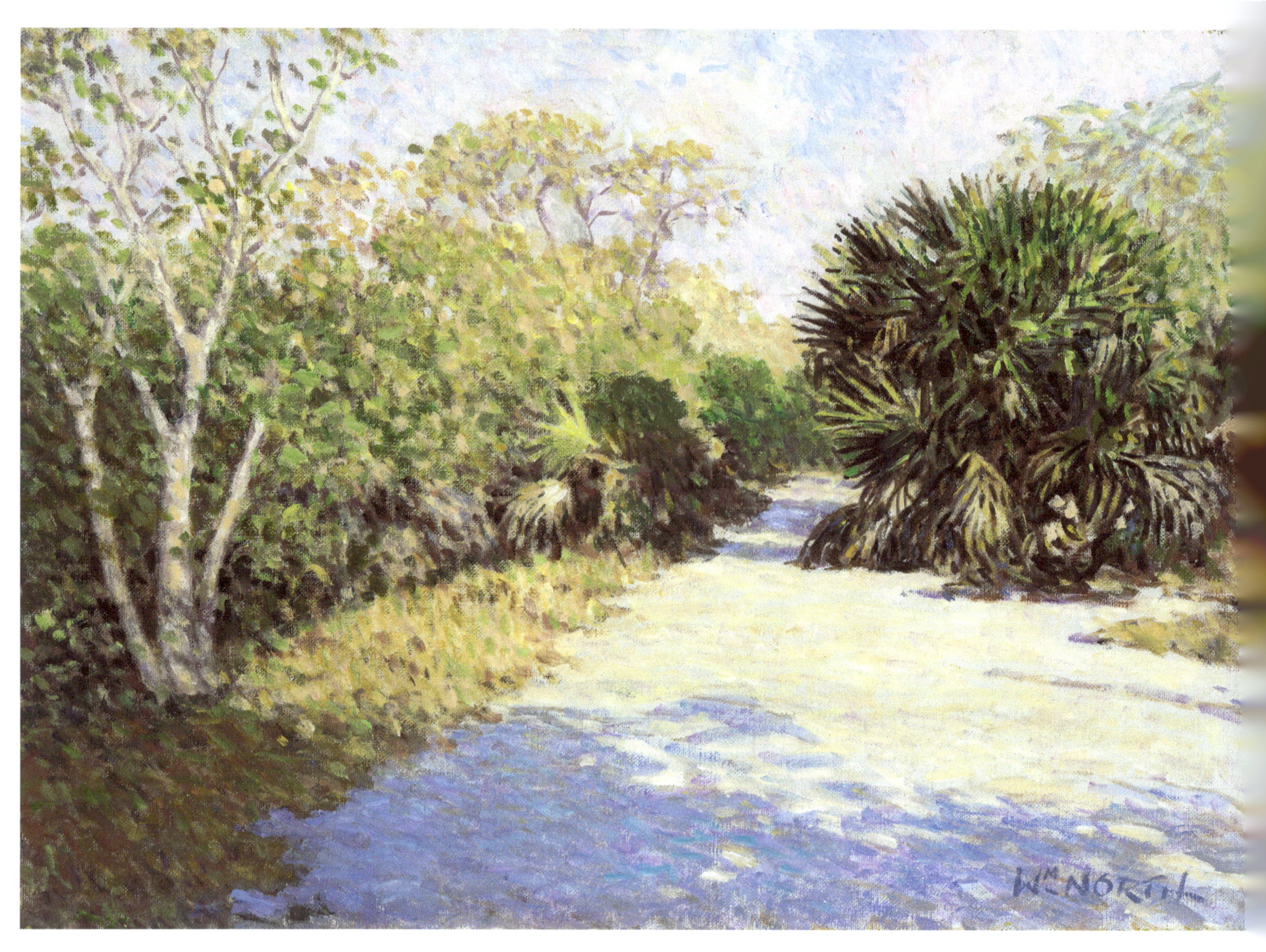

Indigo Trail, Sanibel, FL, Apr. 2002, 12" x 16"

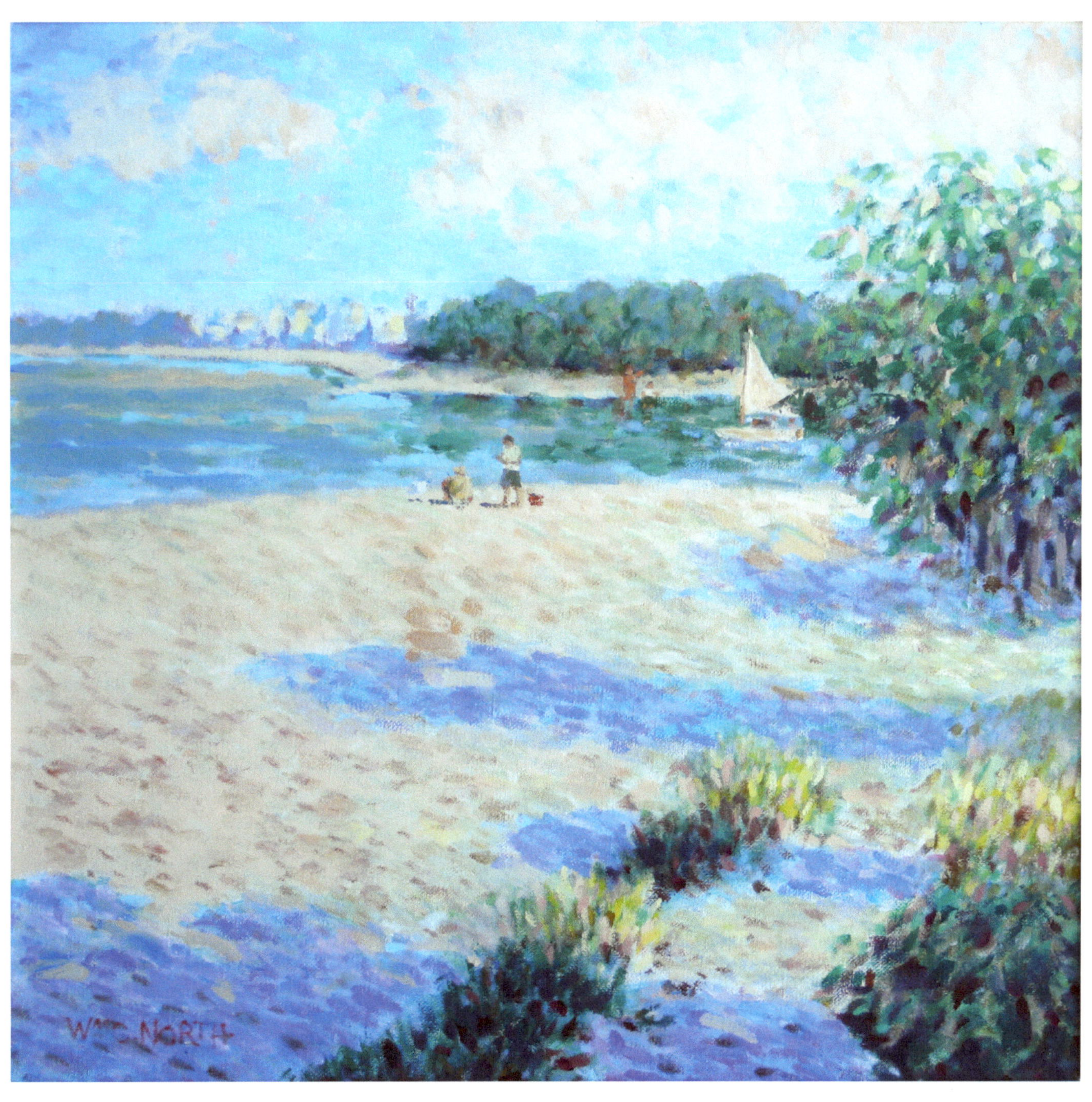

Sailboat in the Pass, Grand Court Studio, Ft. Myers, FL, Jun. 2010, 16" x 16"

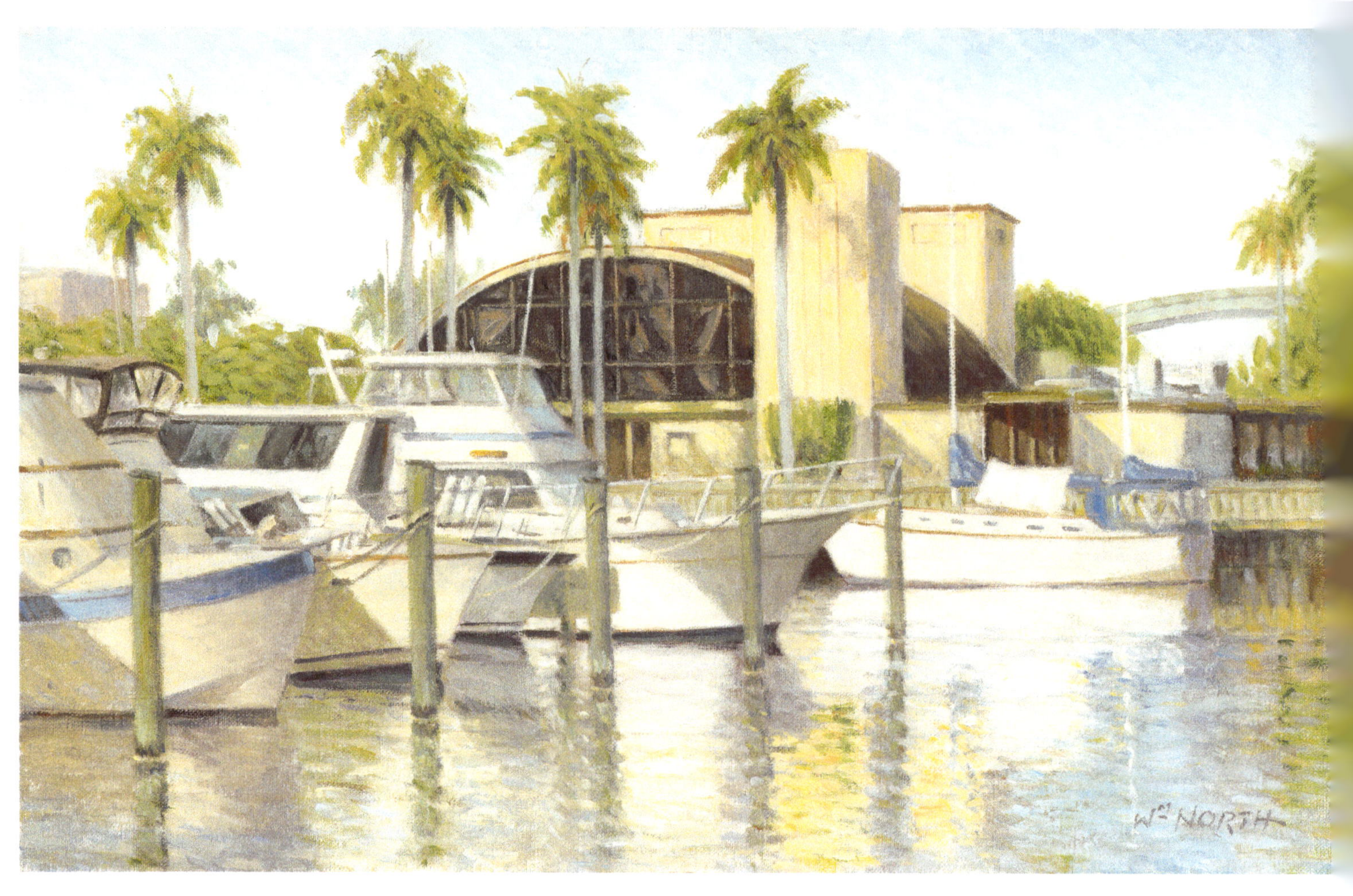

Fort Myers Yacht Basin, Jan. 1998, 9" x 14"

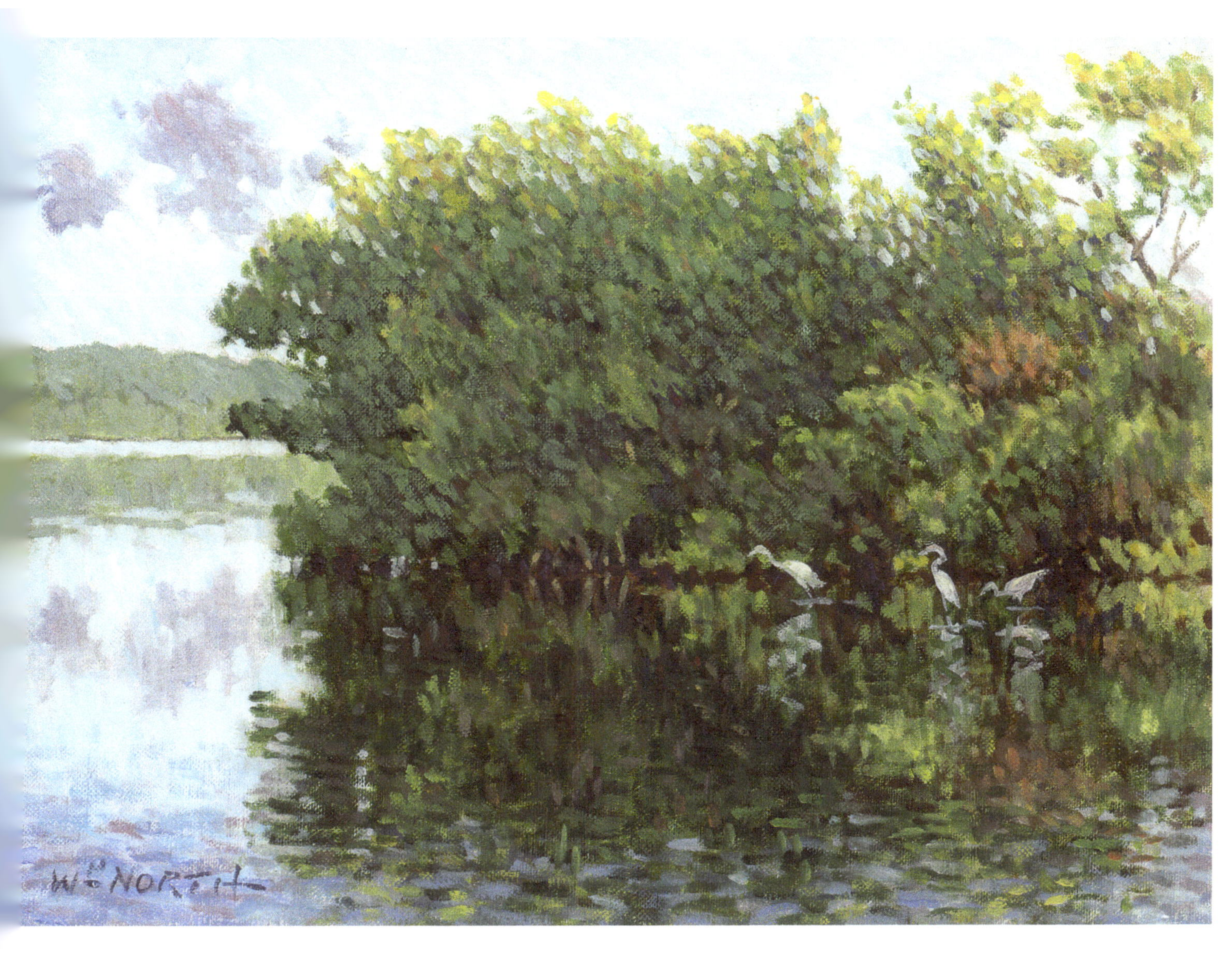

Florida Mangroves, Sanibel, FL, May 2008, 9" x 14"

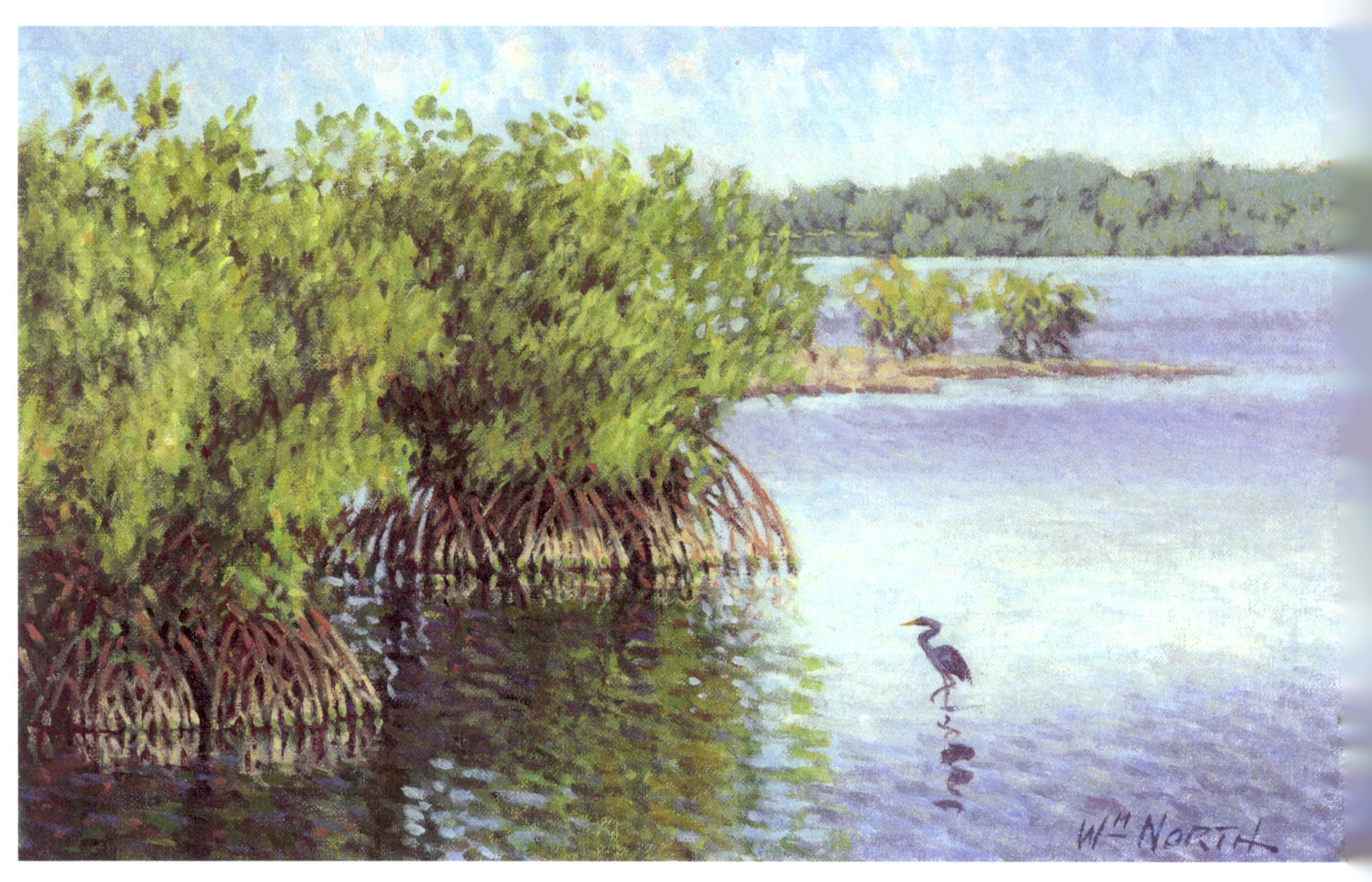

Calusa Indian Walking Tree, Apr. 1998, 9" x 14"

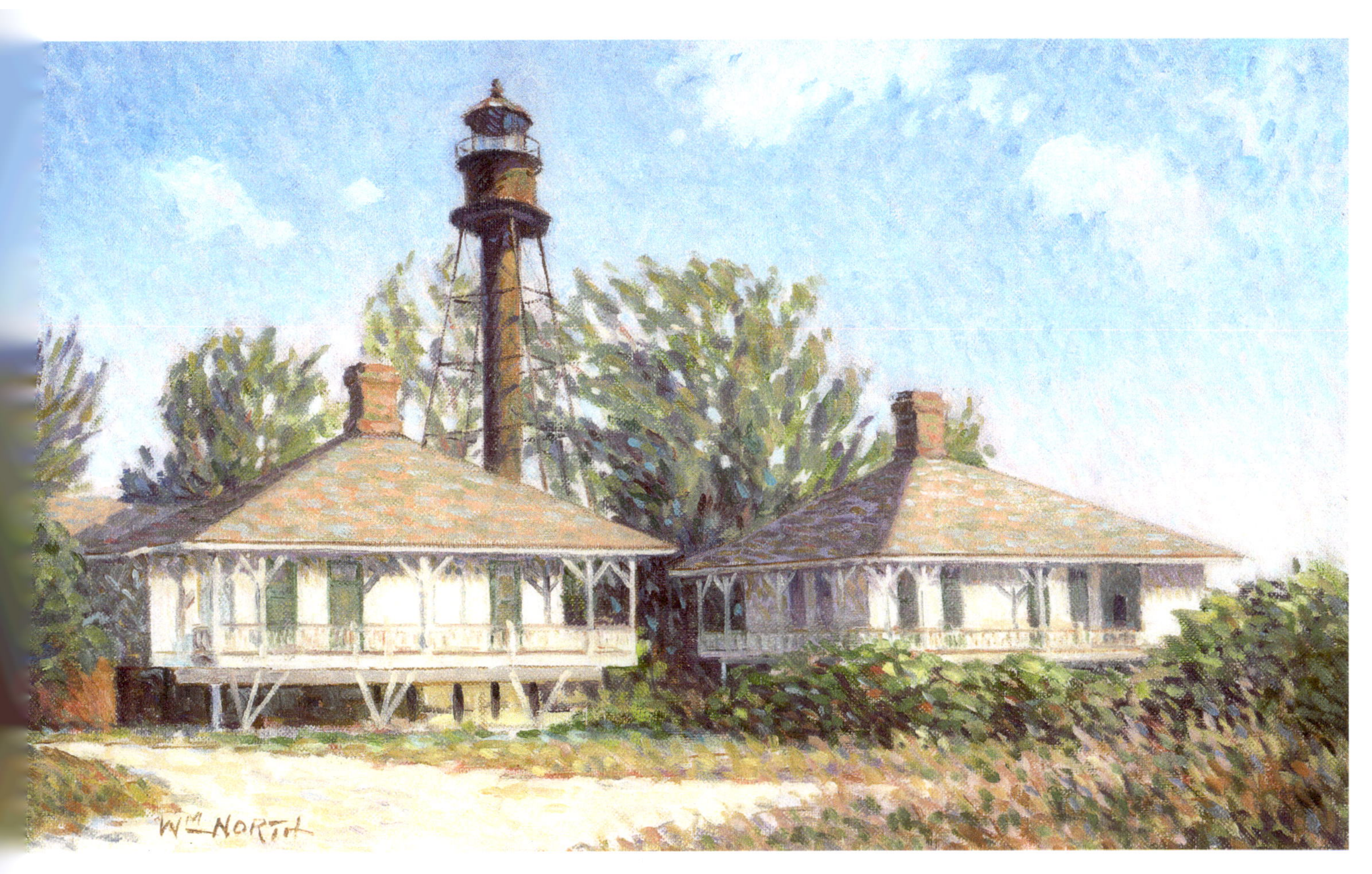

Sanibel Lighthouse, Sanibel, FL, 9" x 14"

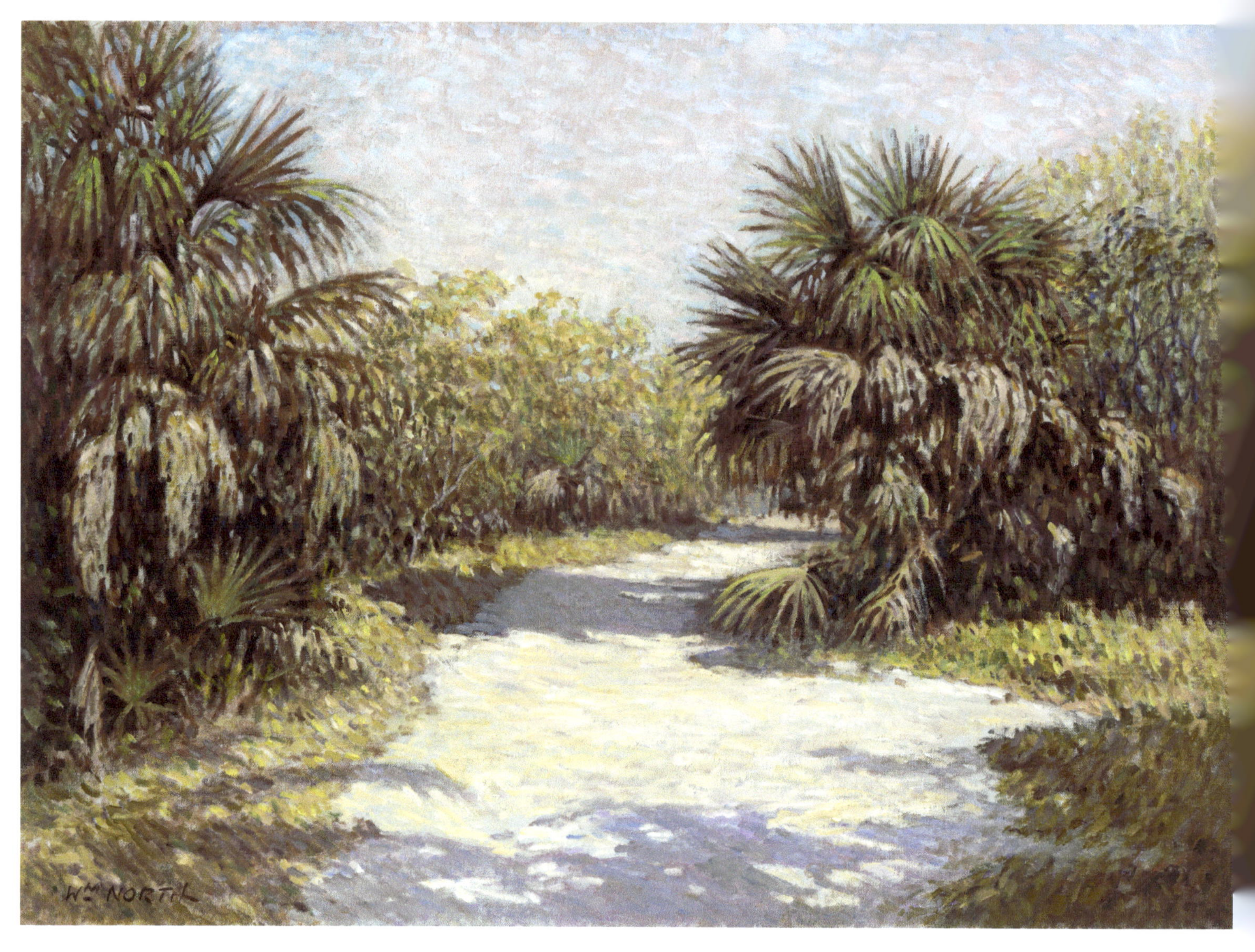

Indigo Trail–Early Morning, Sanibel Island, FL, 9" x 14"

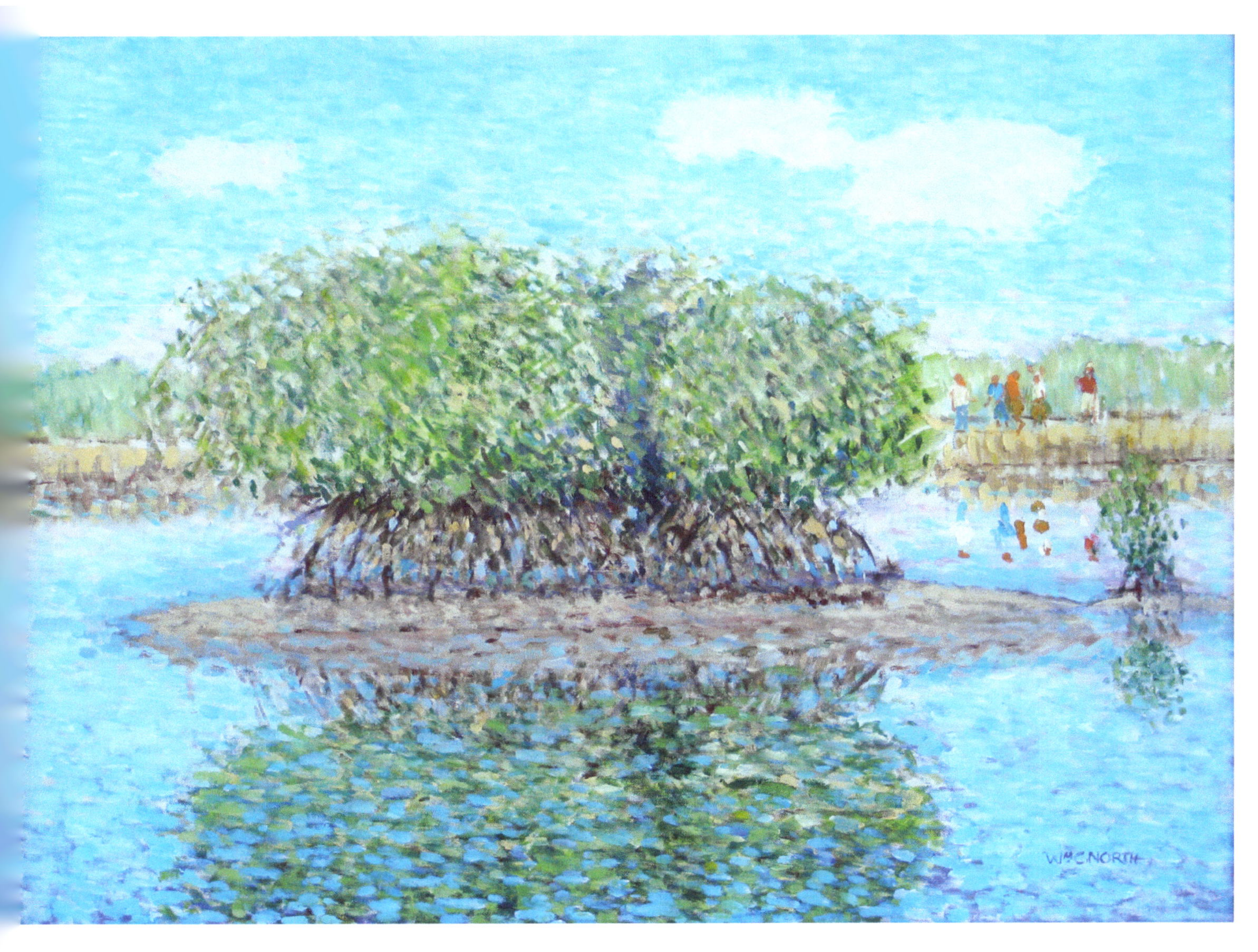

Impressionist Mangrove, Grand Court Studio, Ft. Myers, FL, Oct. 2010, 18" x 24"

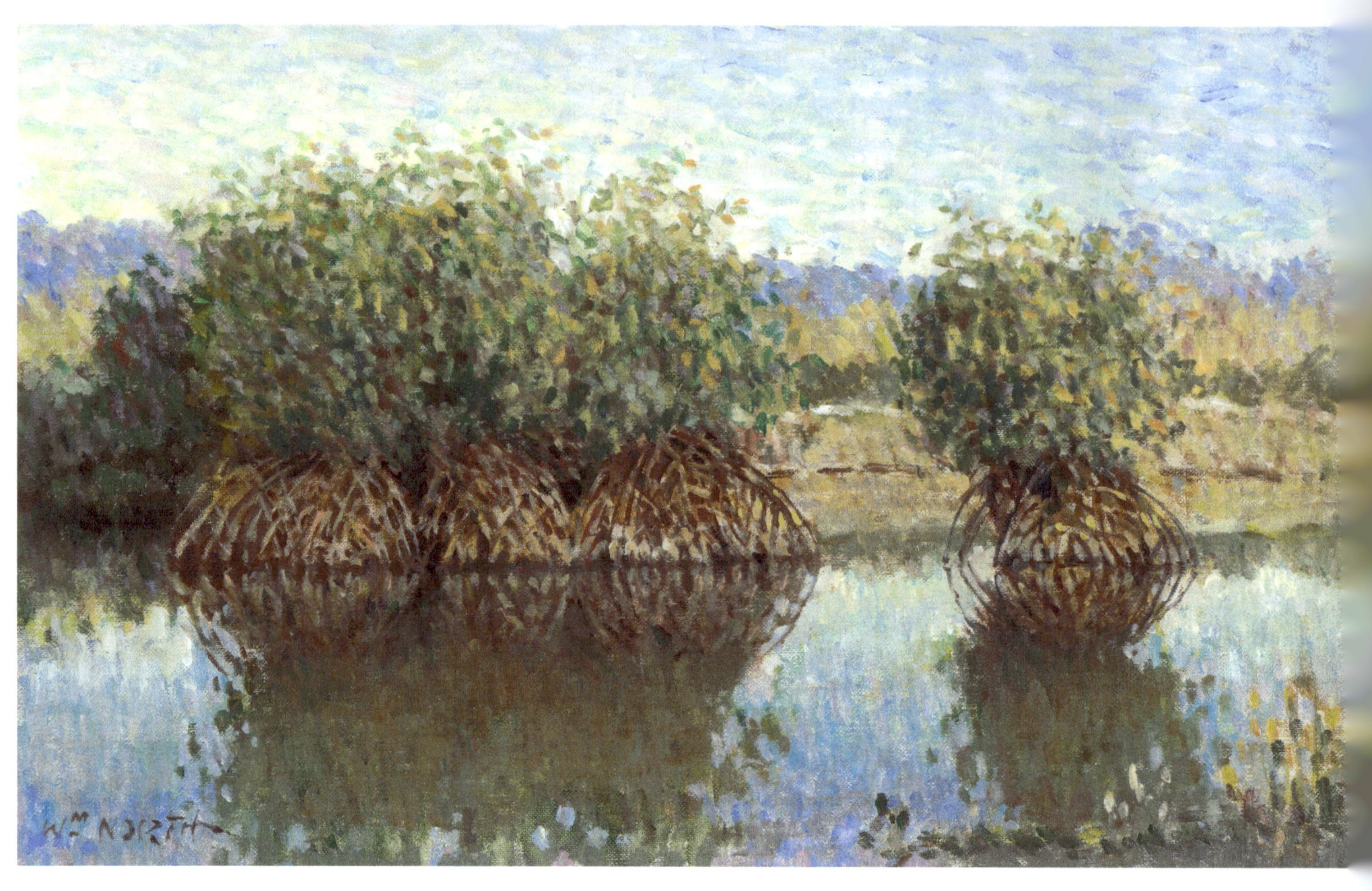

Mangrove Island, Sanibel Island, FL, 9" x 14"

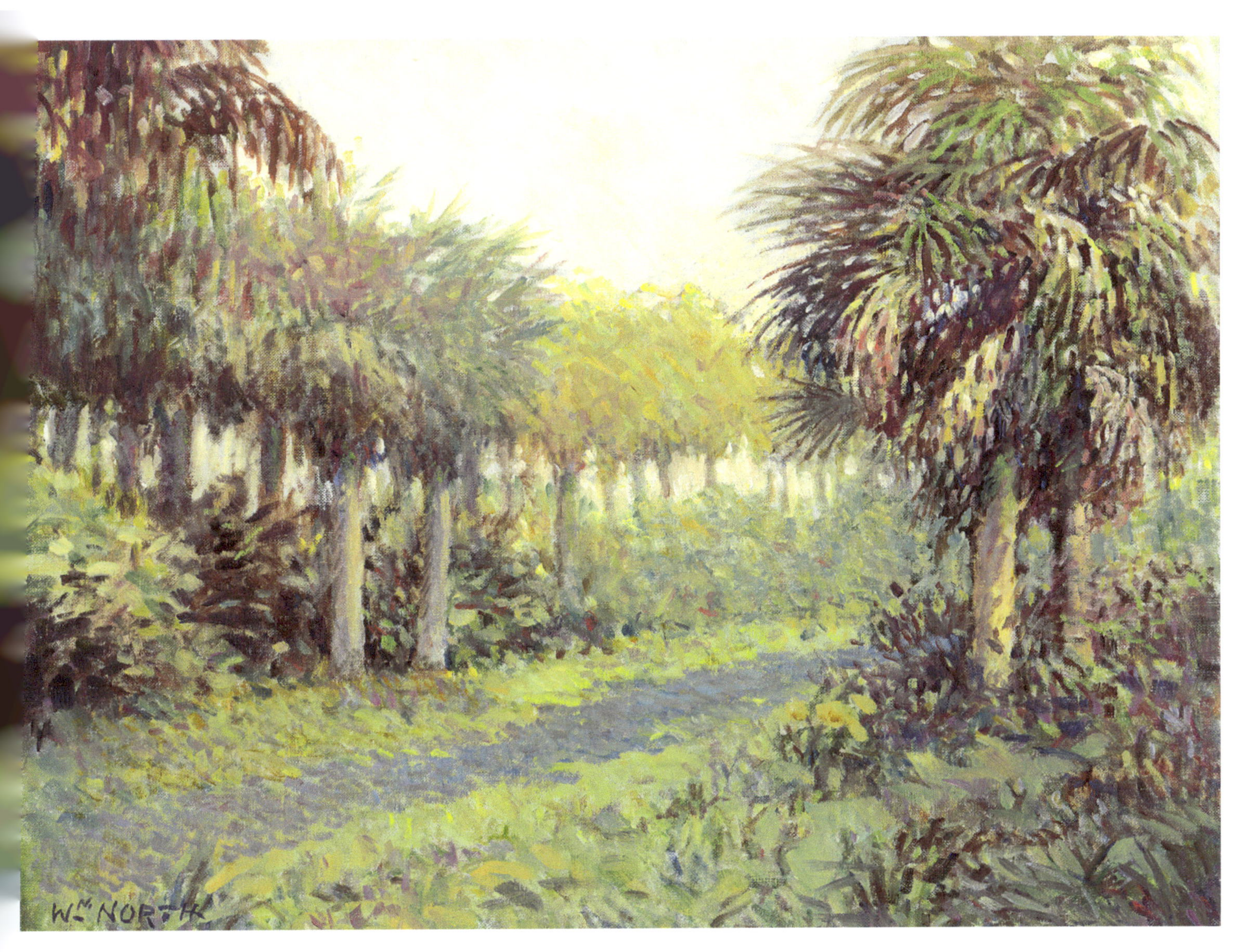

Ding Darling Indigo Trail on a Misty Day, Sanibel Island, FL, 9" x 14"

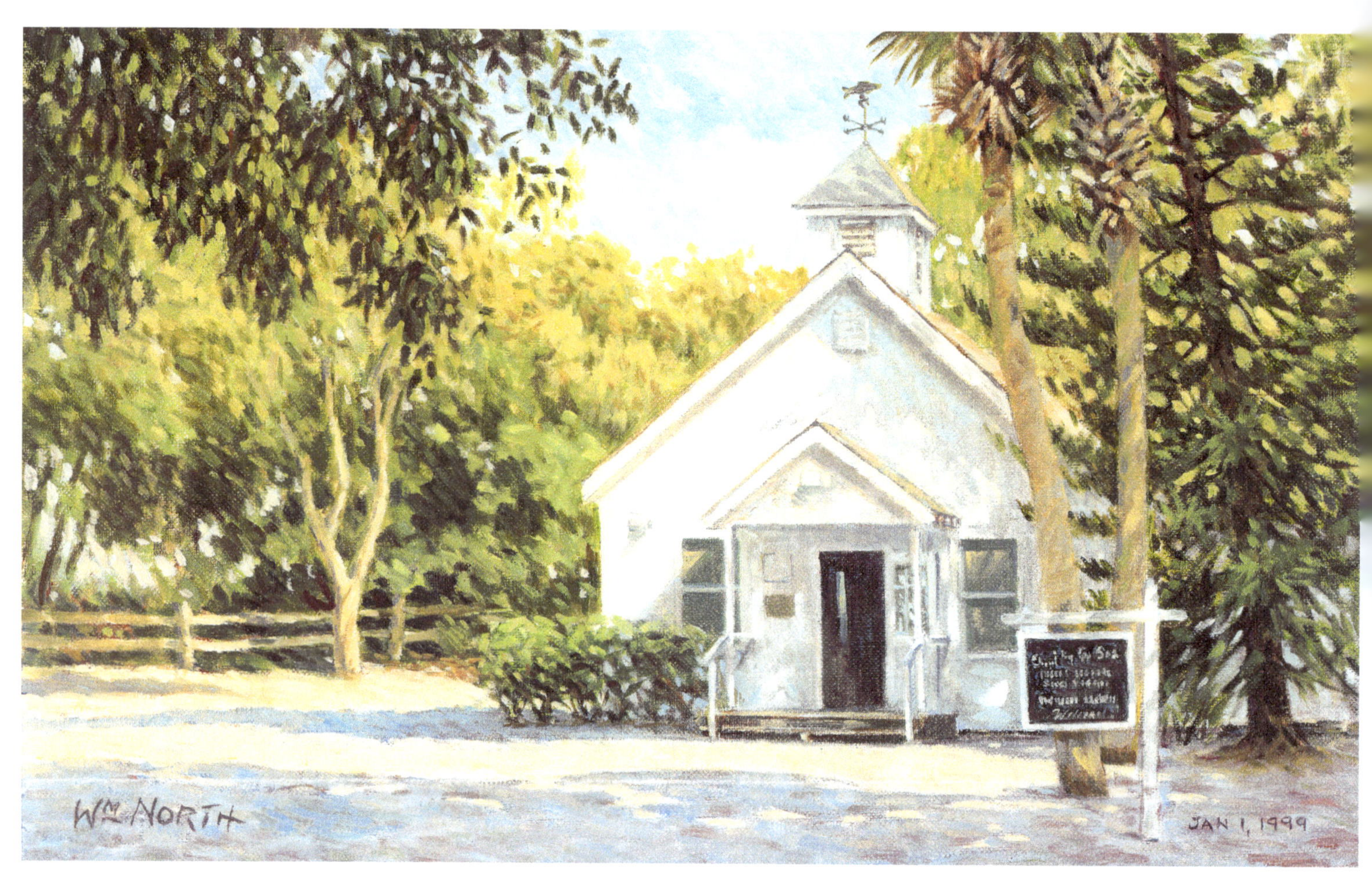

Chapel by the Sea in Summer, Captiva Island, FL, Jul. 1998, 9" x 14"

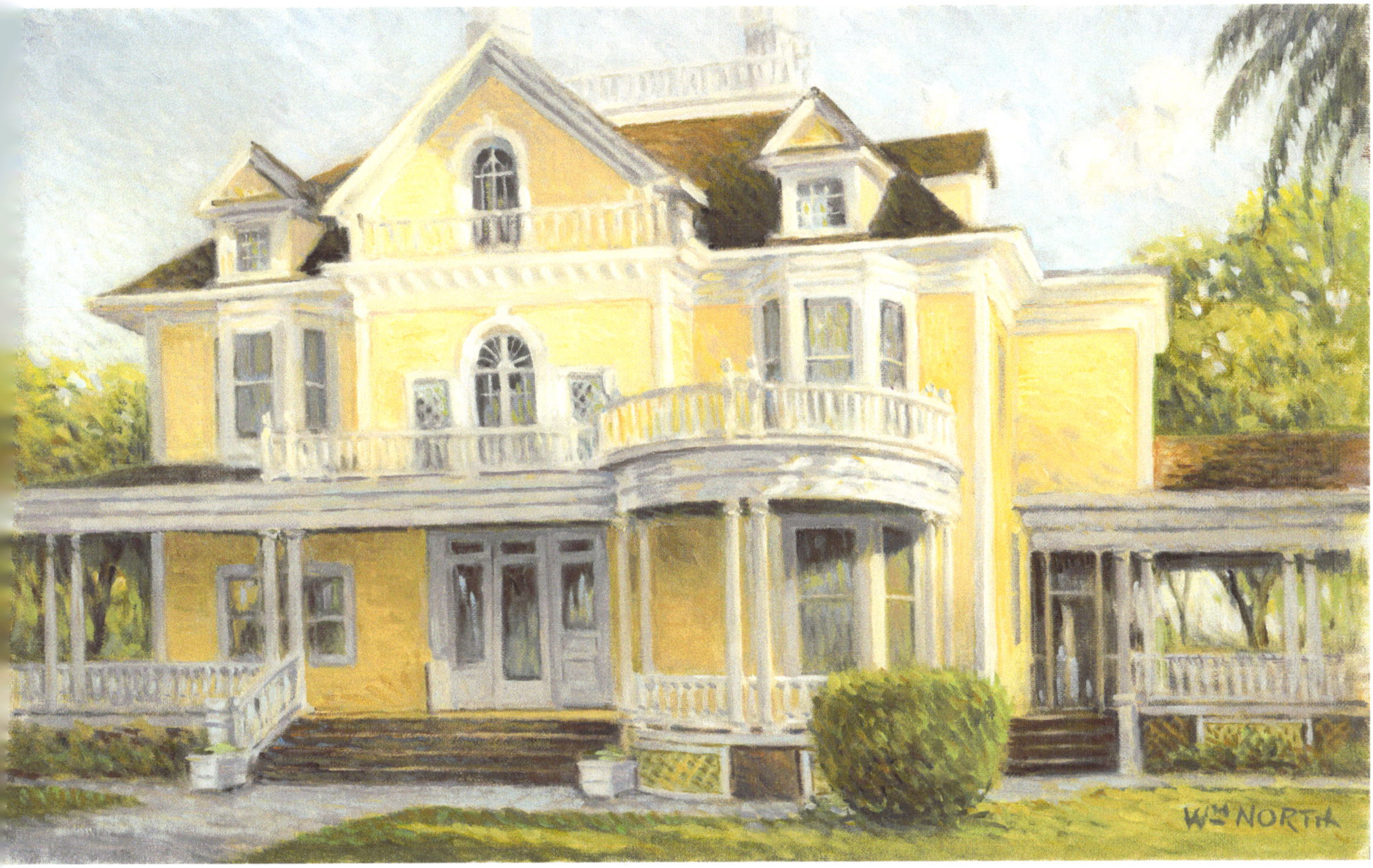

Burroughs Home, Ft. Myers, FL, Jun. 2000, 11" x 17"

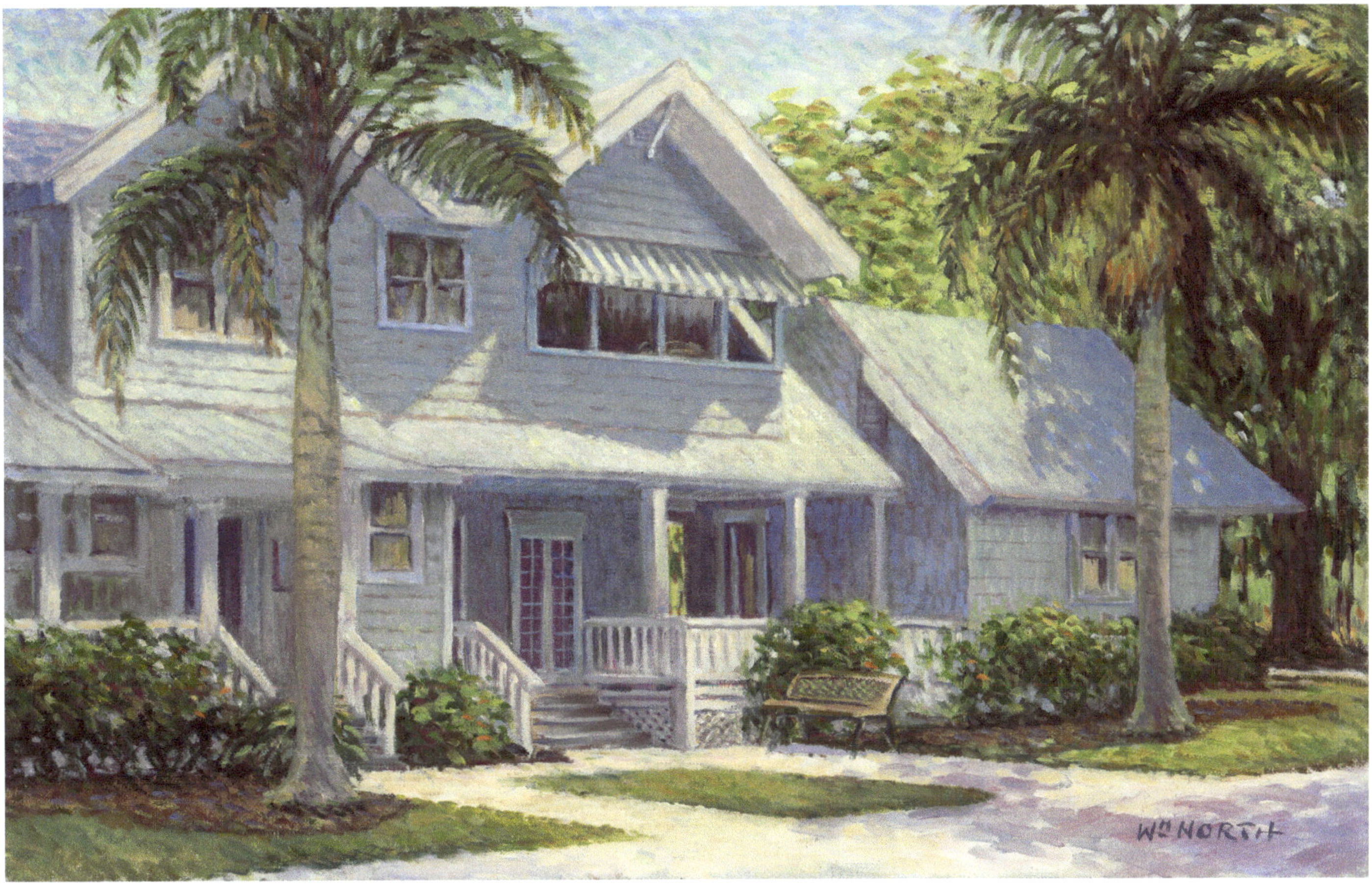

Henry Ford Winter Home, Edison Museum, Ft. Myers, FL, Sep. 2000, 11" x 17"

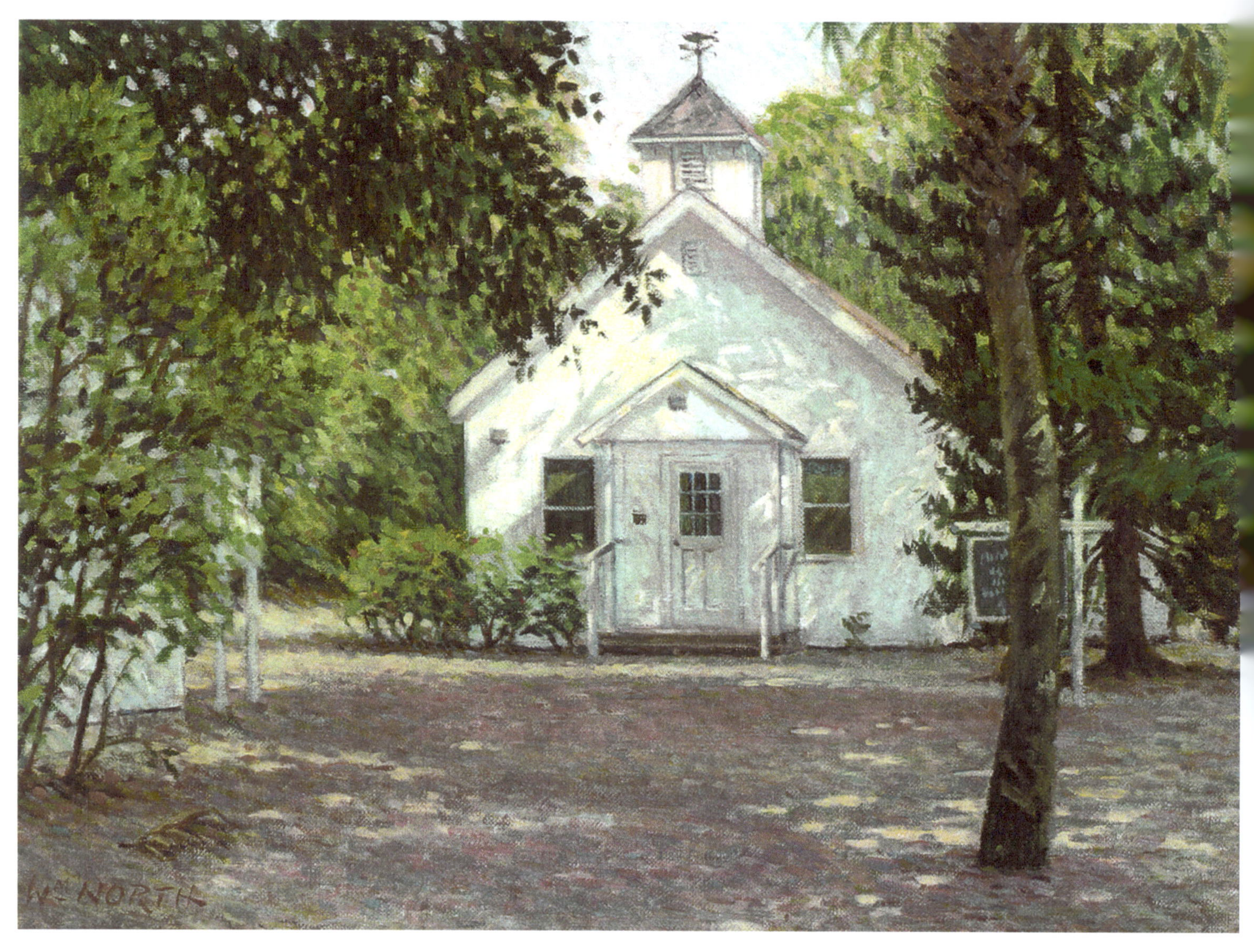

Chapel by the Sea in Fall, Captiva Island, FL, 1999, 9" x 14"

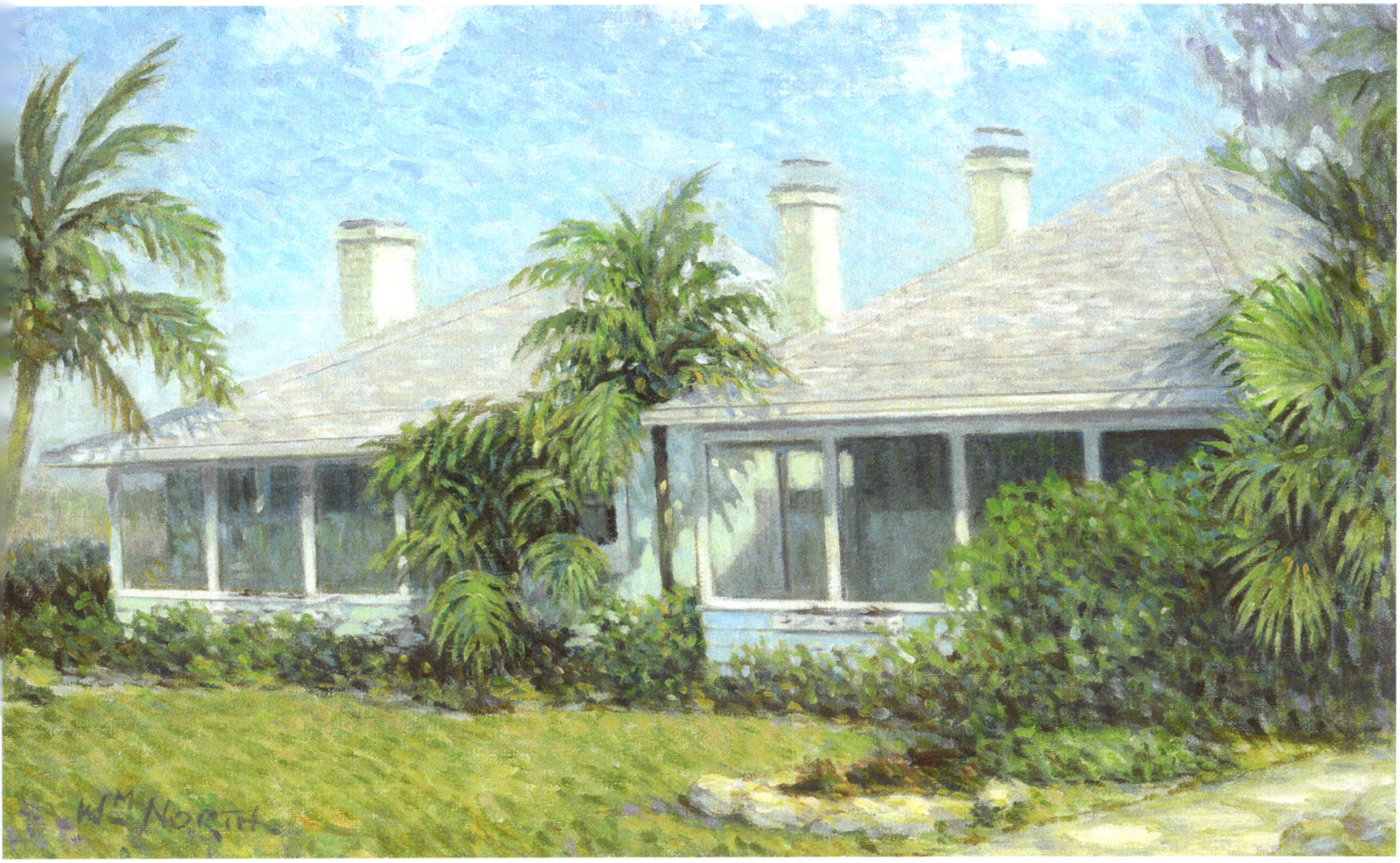

Lindberg Cottages, 'Tween Waters, Captiva Island, FL, Nov. 2001, 11" x 17"

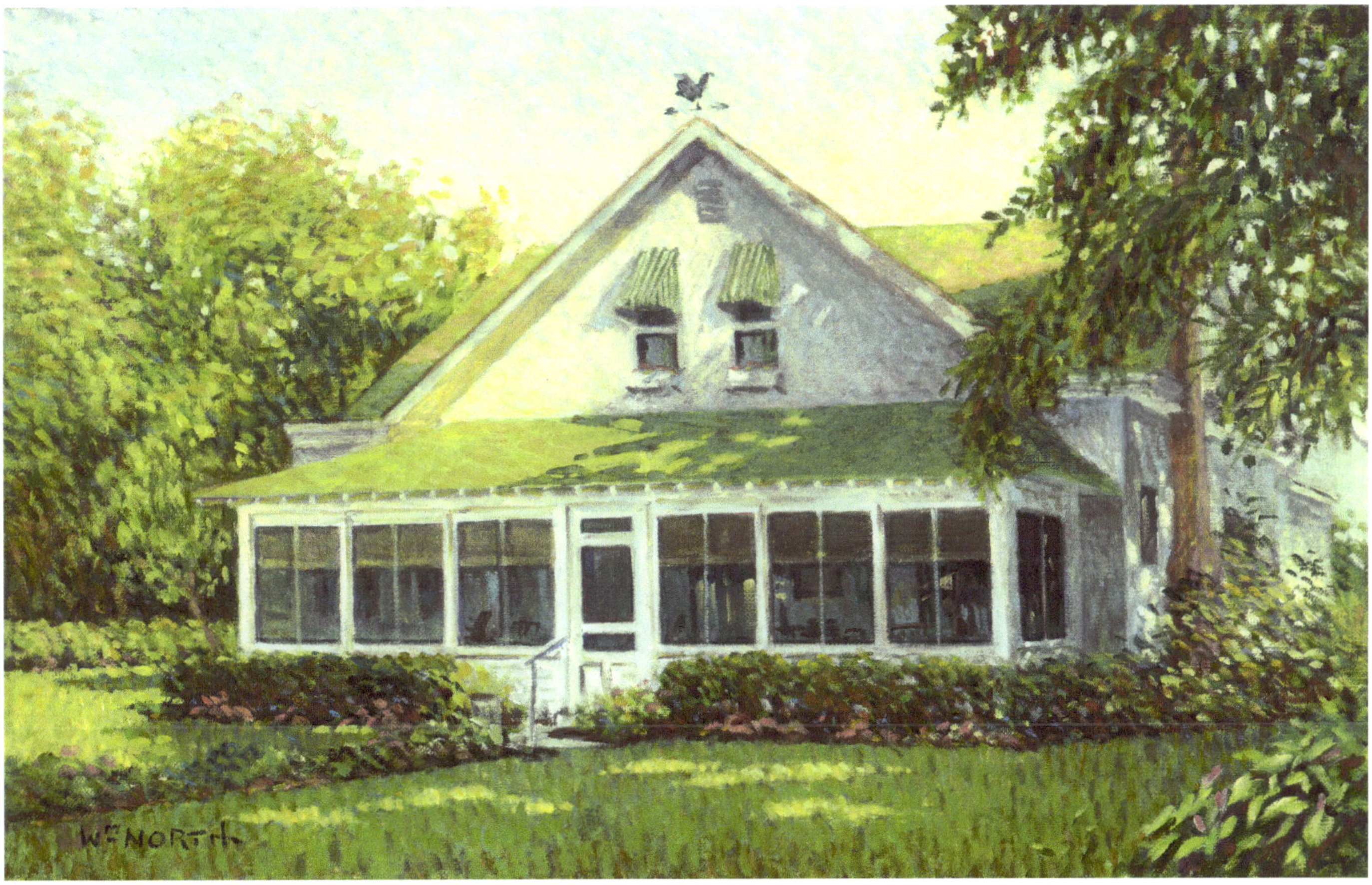

Historic Palm Cottage, Naples, FL, Jul. 1999, 11" x 17"

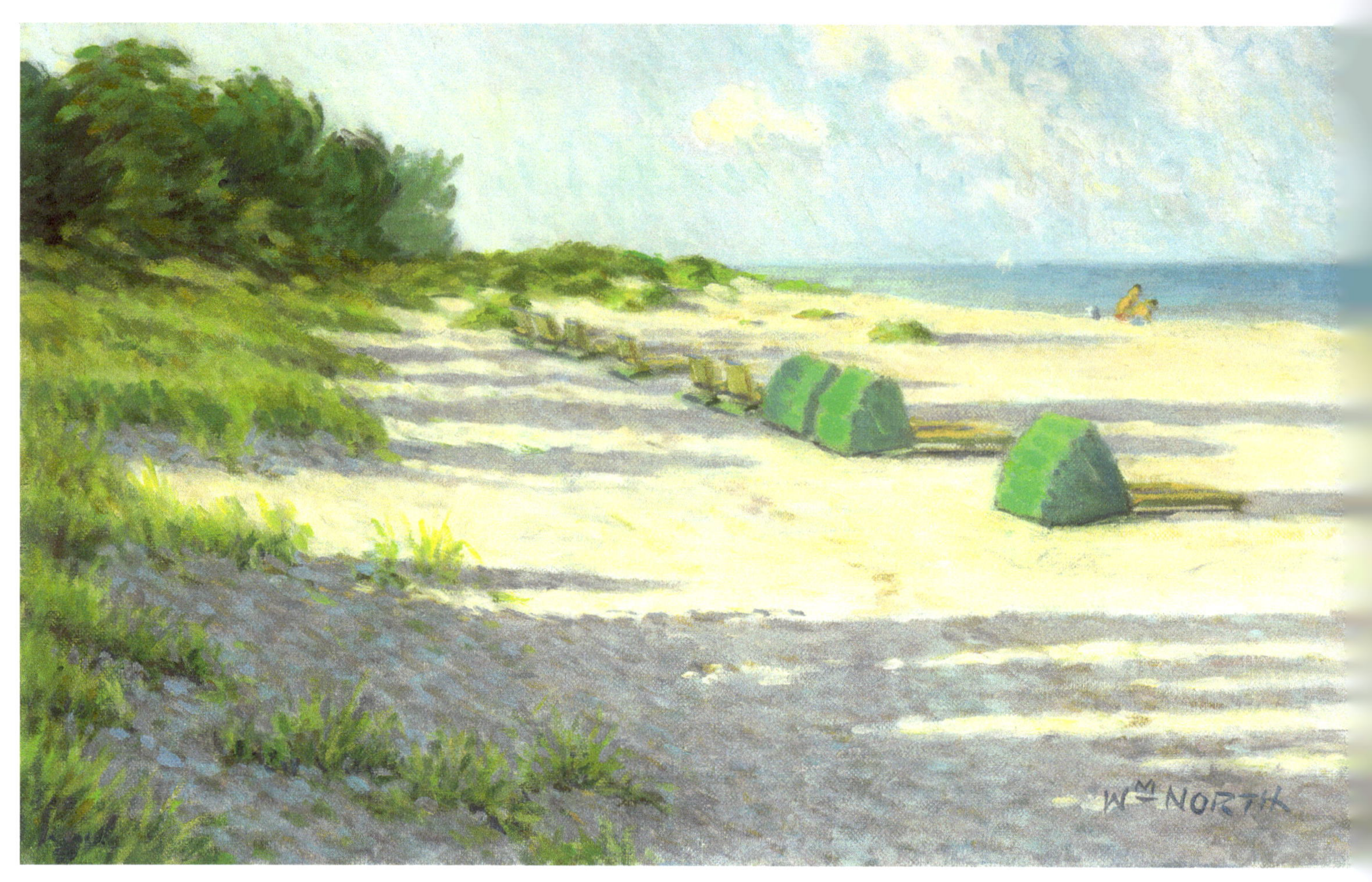

'Tween Waters Beach, Captiva Island, FL, 1997, 9" x 14"

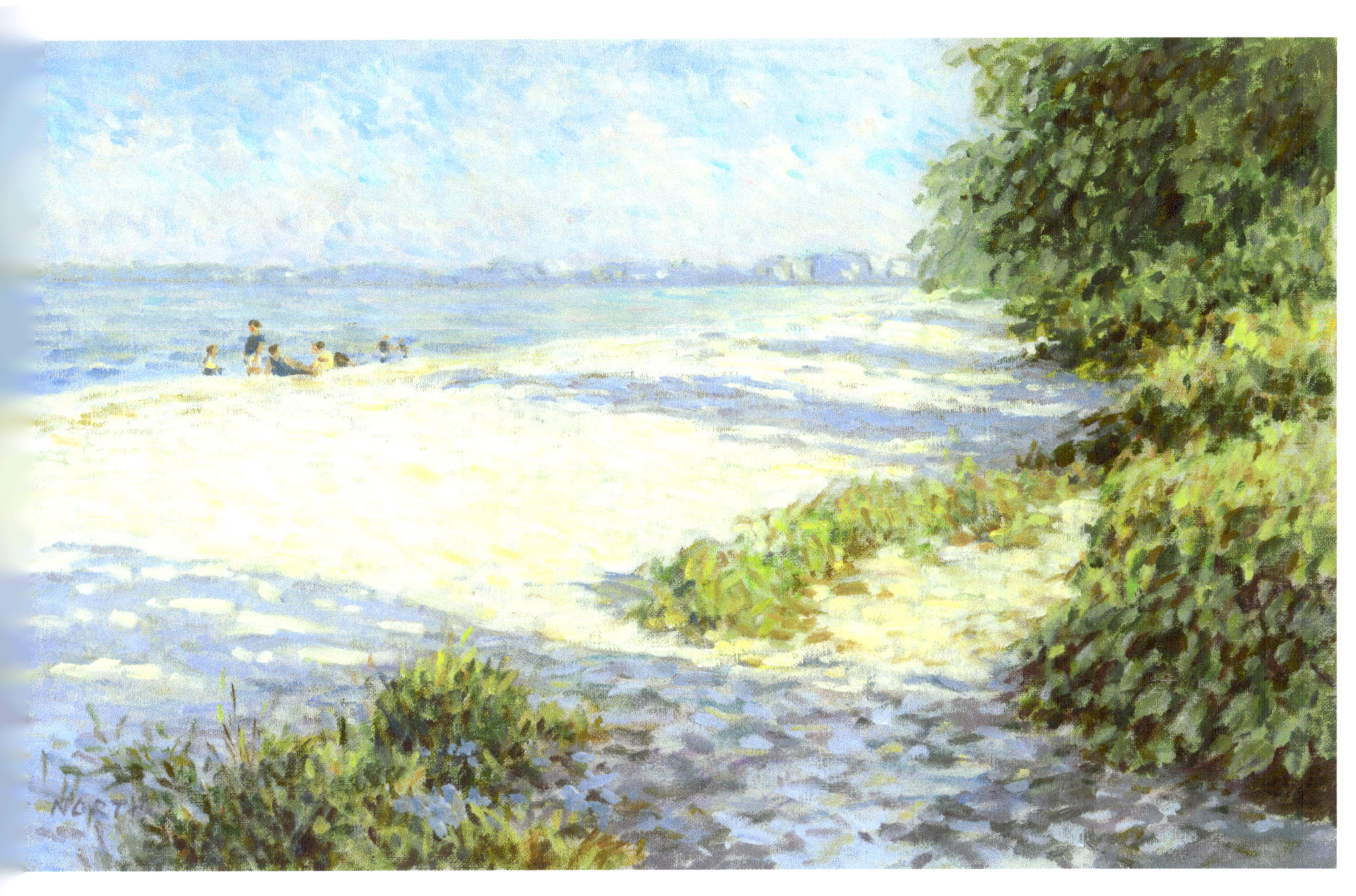

My Favorite Beach, Wiggins Pass State Park, Naples, FL, Jan. 2003, 11" x 17"

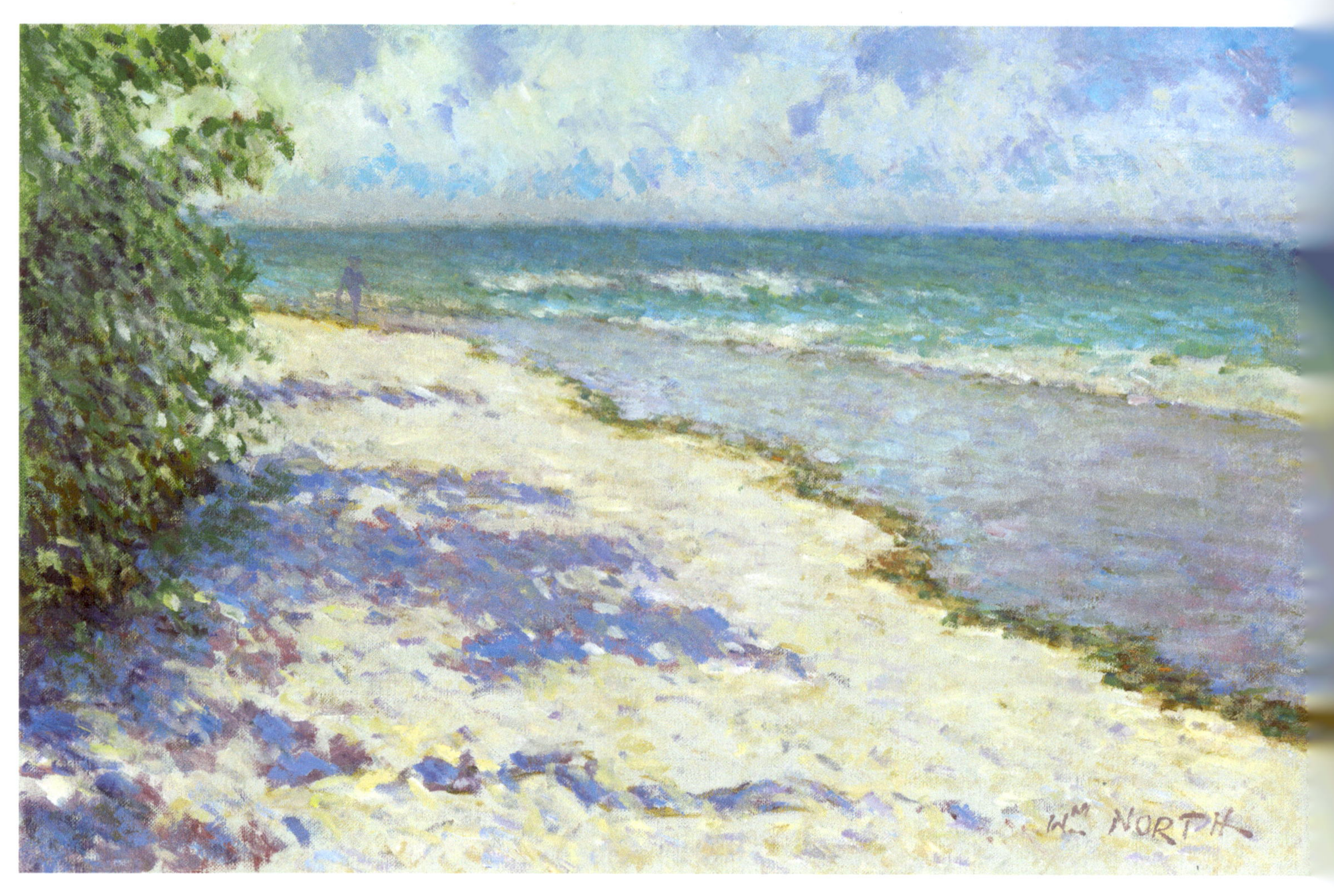

Ebb Tide, Delnor-Wiggins Pass State Park, looking south, 9" x 14"

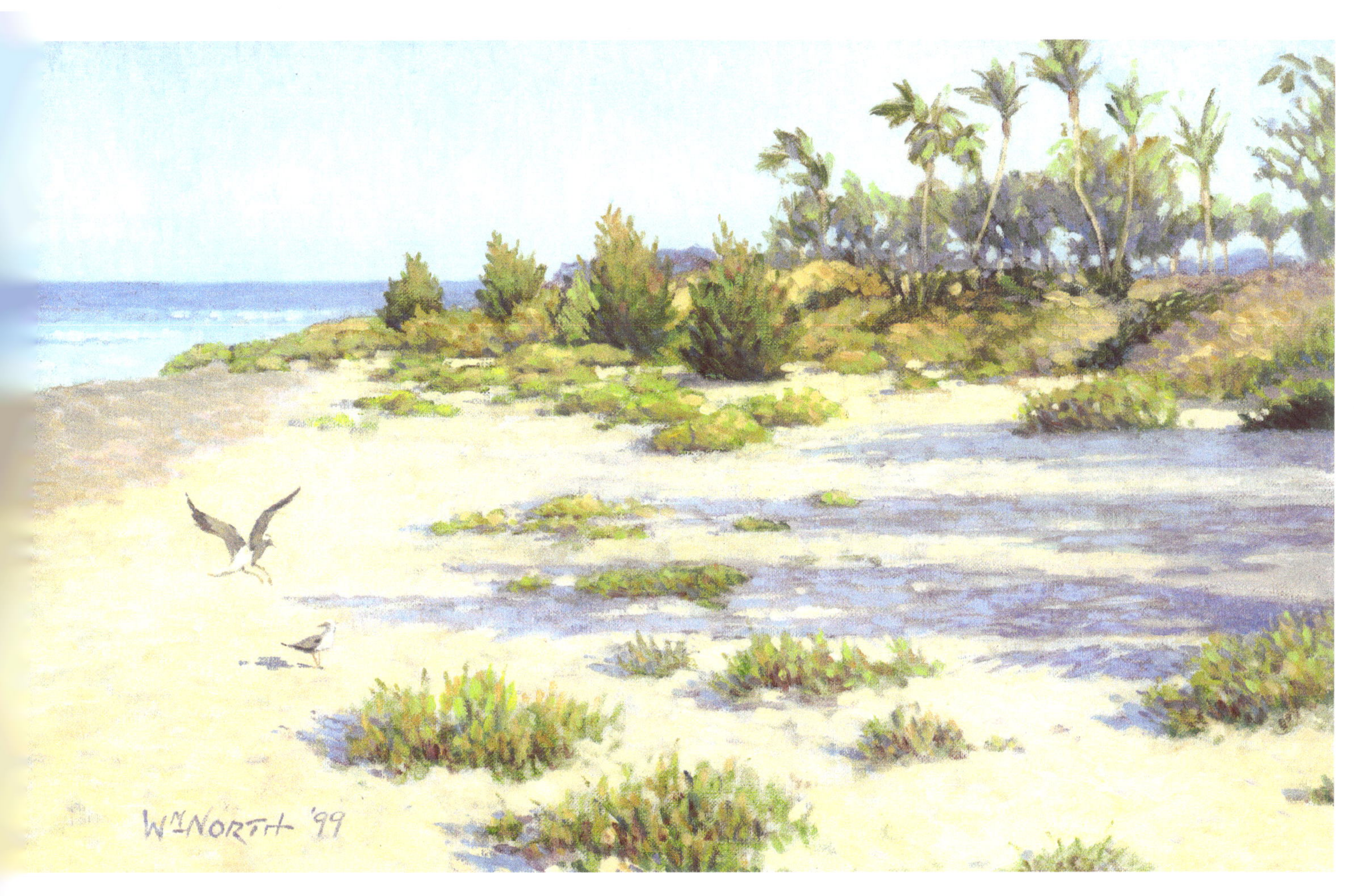

Sunset Beach at Sunrise, Captiva Island, FL, Mar. 1999, 11" x 17"

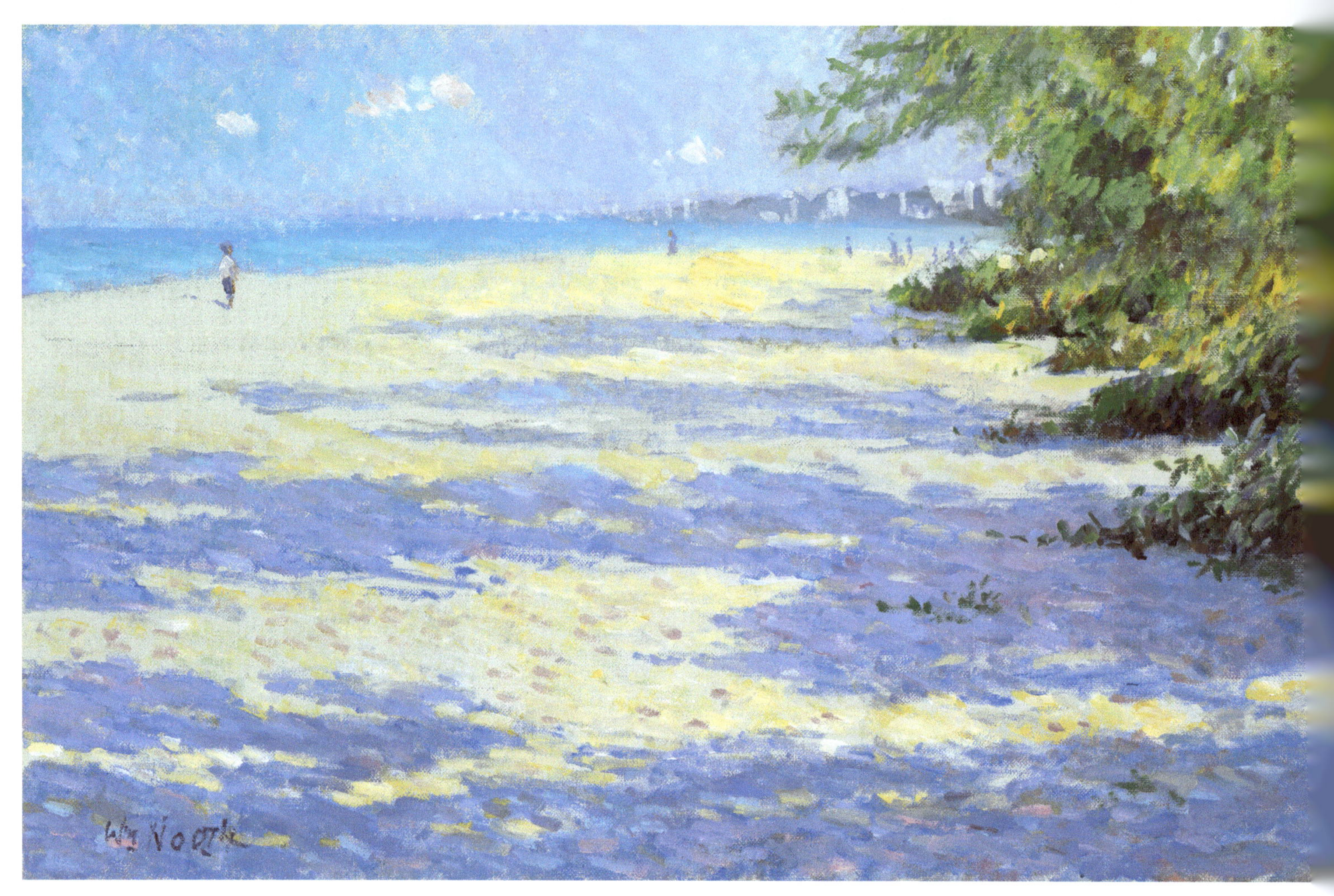

Shadows on the Sand, Wiggins Beach, Naples, FL, Nov. 1999, 9" x 14"

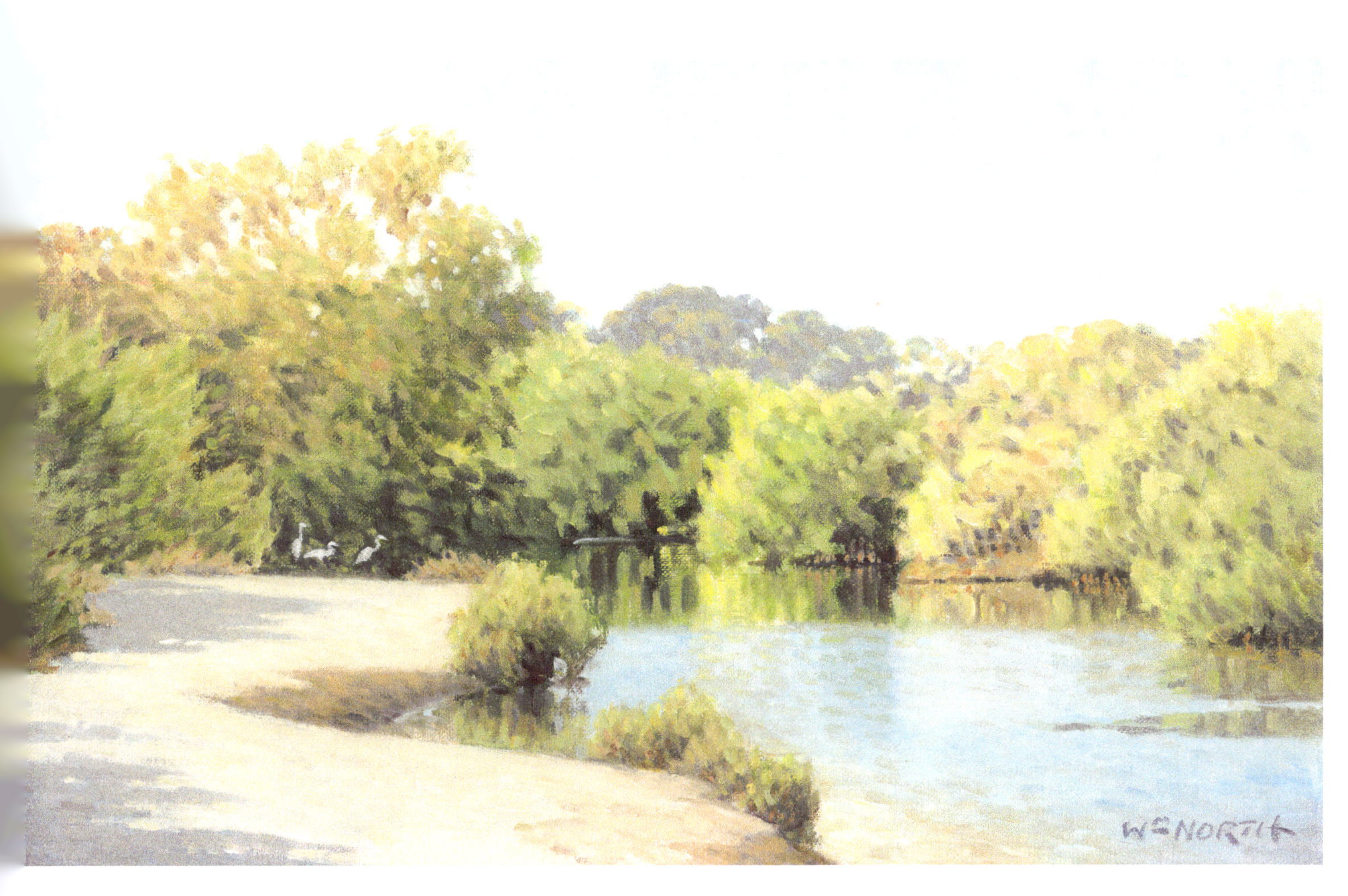

Ding Darling Wildlife, Sanibel Island, FL, May 1998, 9" x 14"

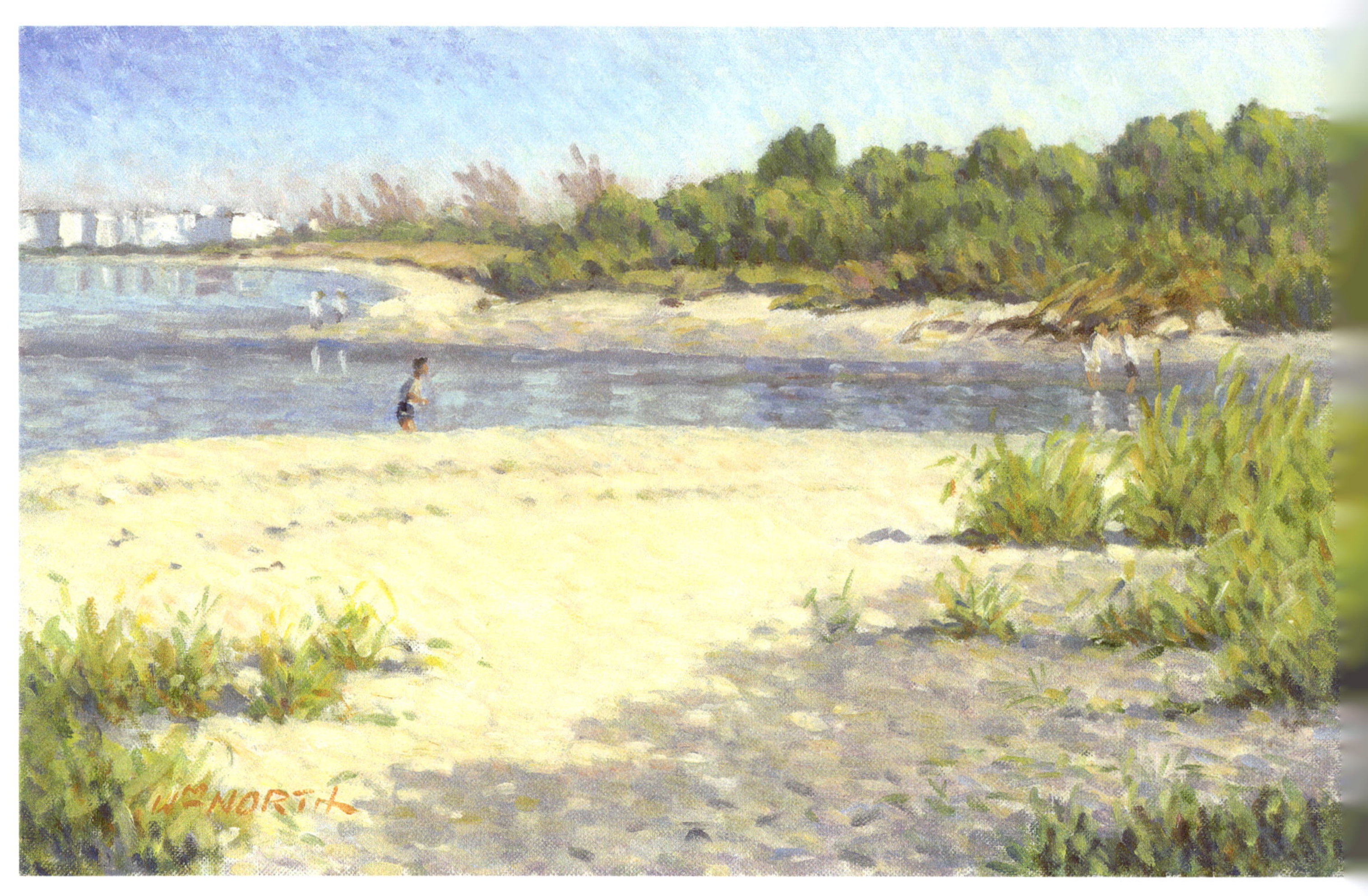

Running Man, Wiggins Beach, Naples, FL, Nov. 1999, 9" x 14"

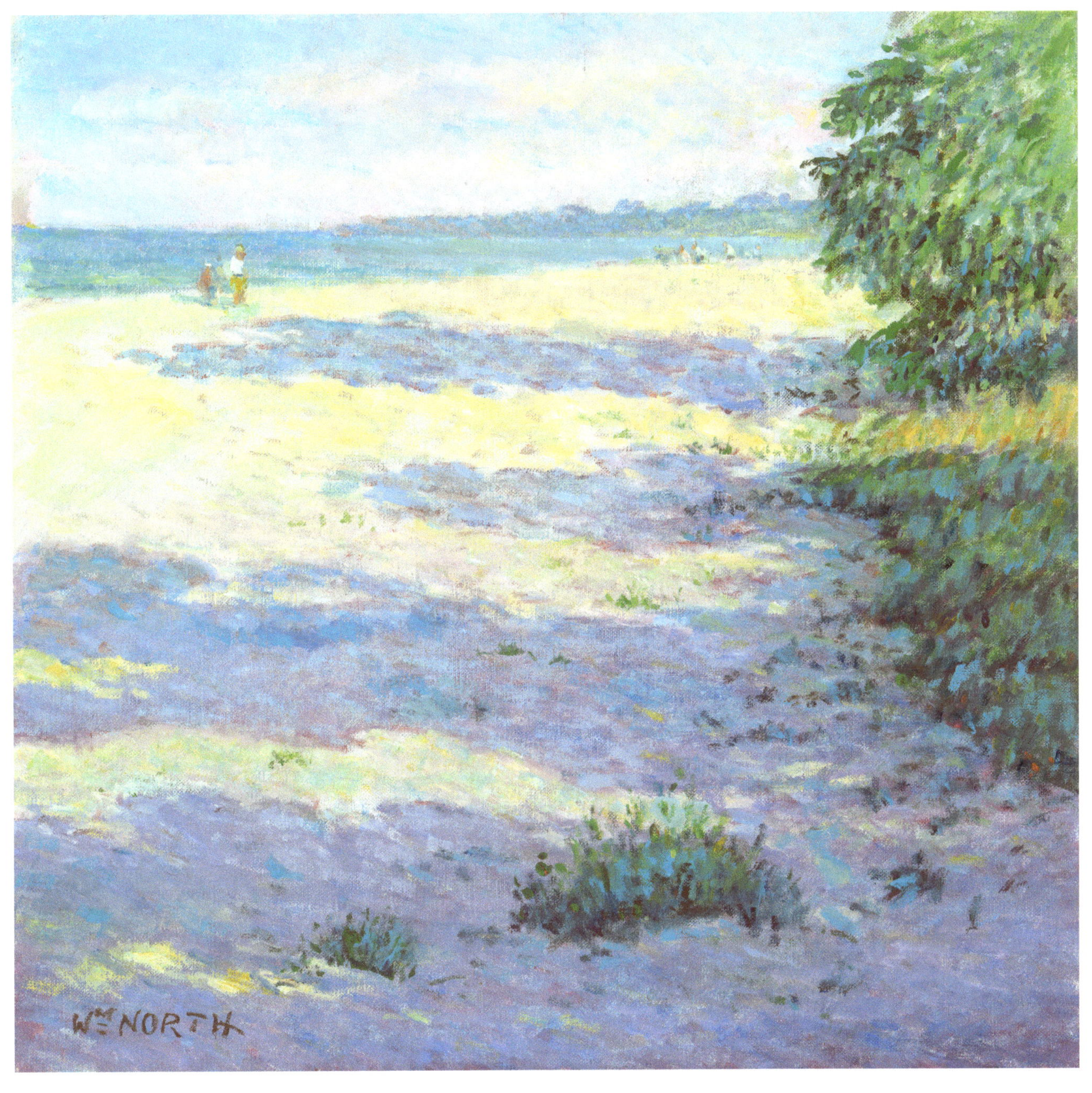

Morning Shadows, Wiggins Beach, Naples, FL, Jan. 2007, 16" x 16"

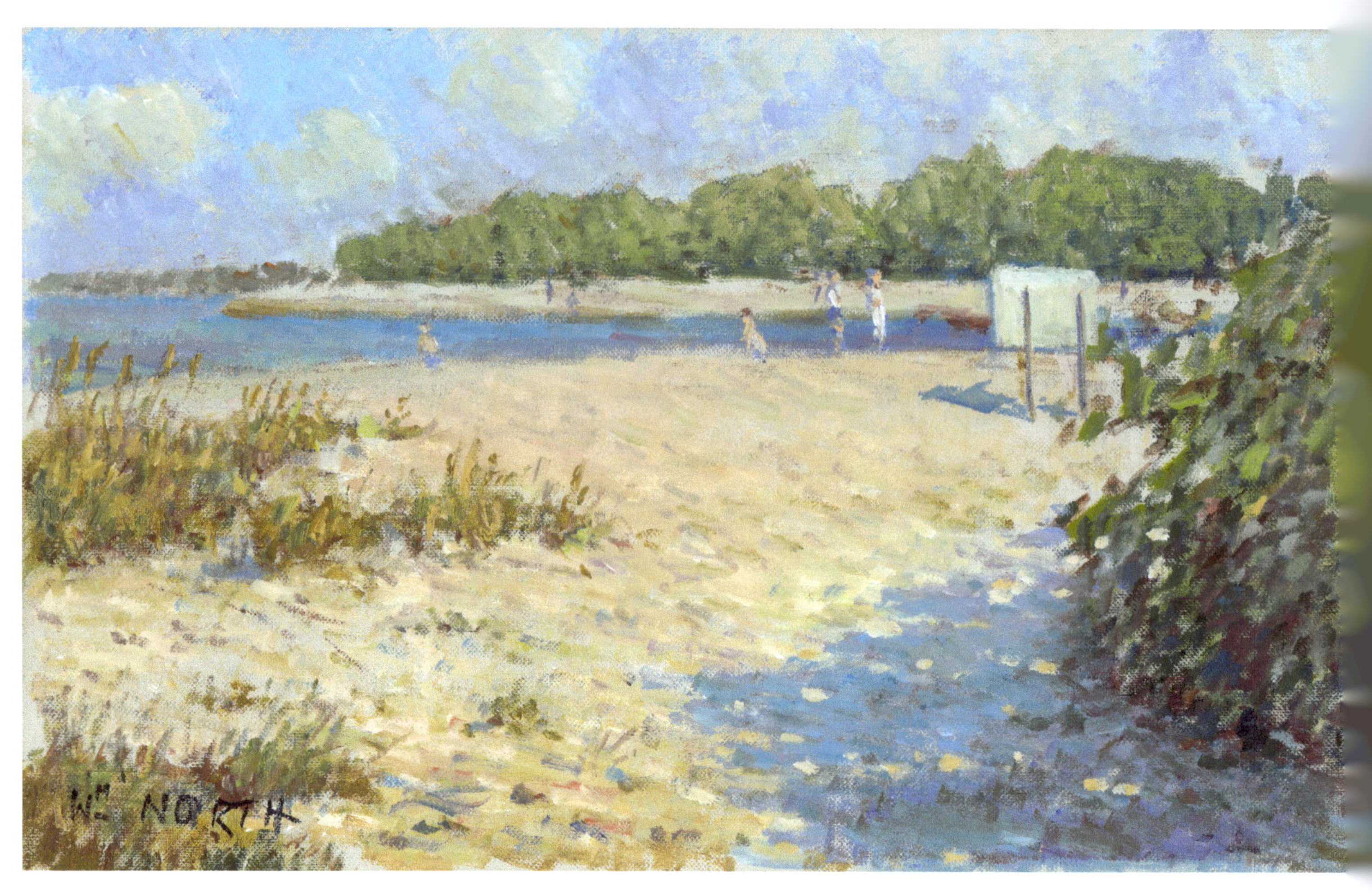

Delnor-Wiggins Pass, Naples, FL, Apr. 2007, 9" x 14"

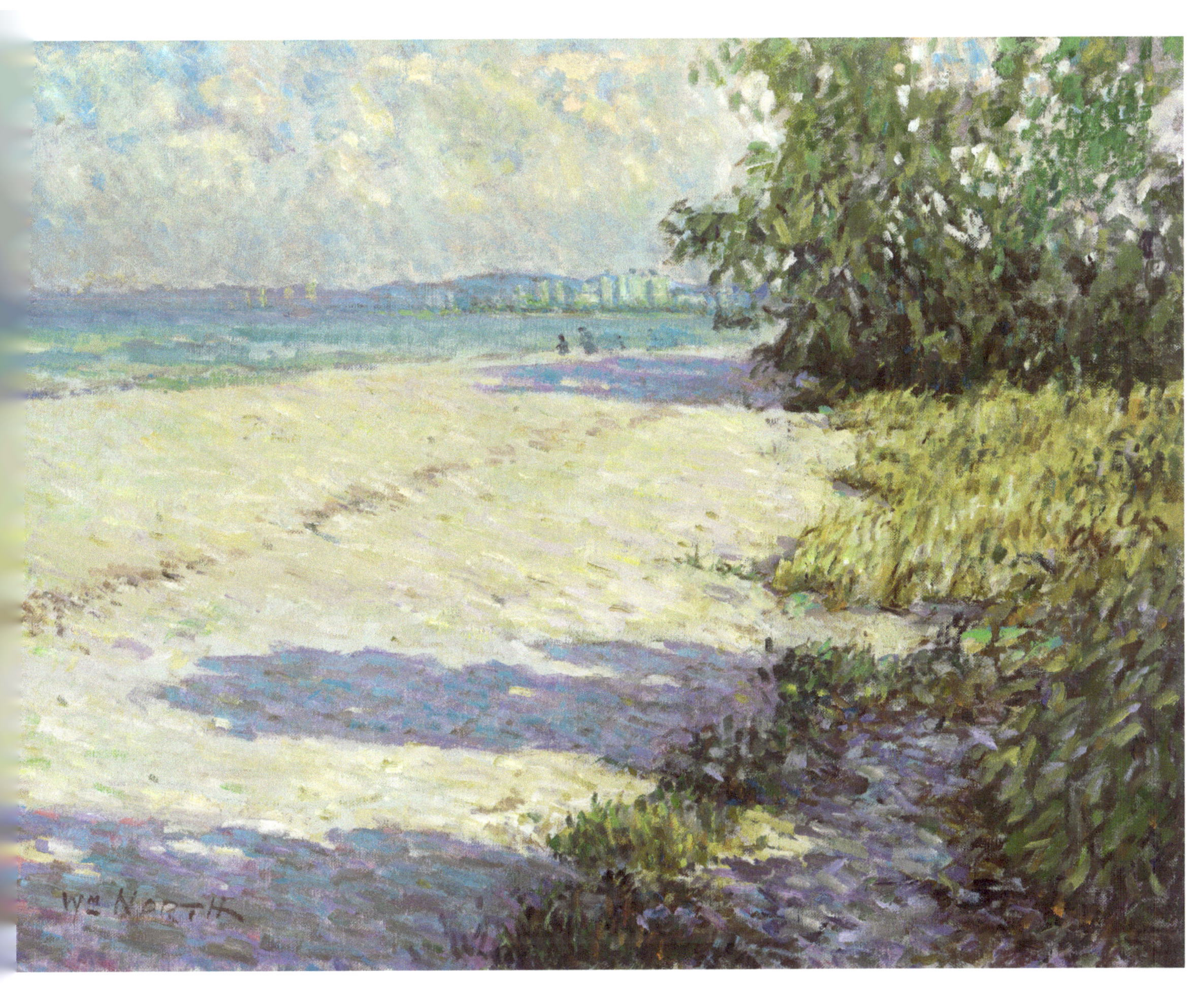

Sunlit Beach–Delnor-Wiggins Pass State Park, Naples, FL, Jan. 2007, 16" x 20"

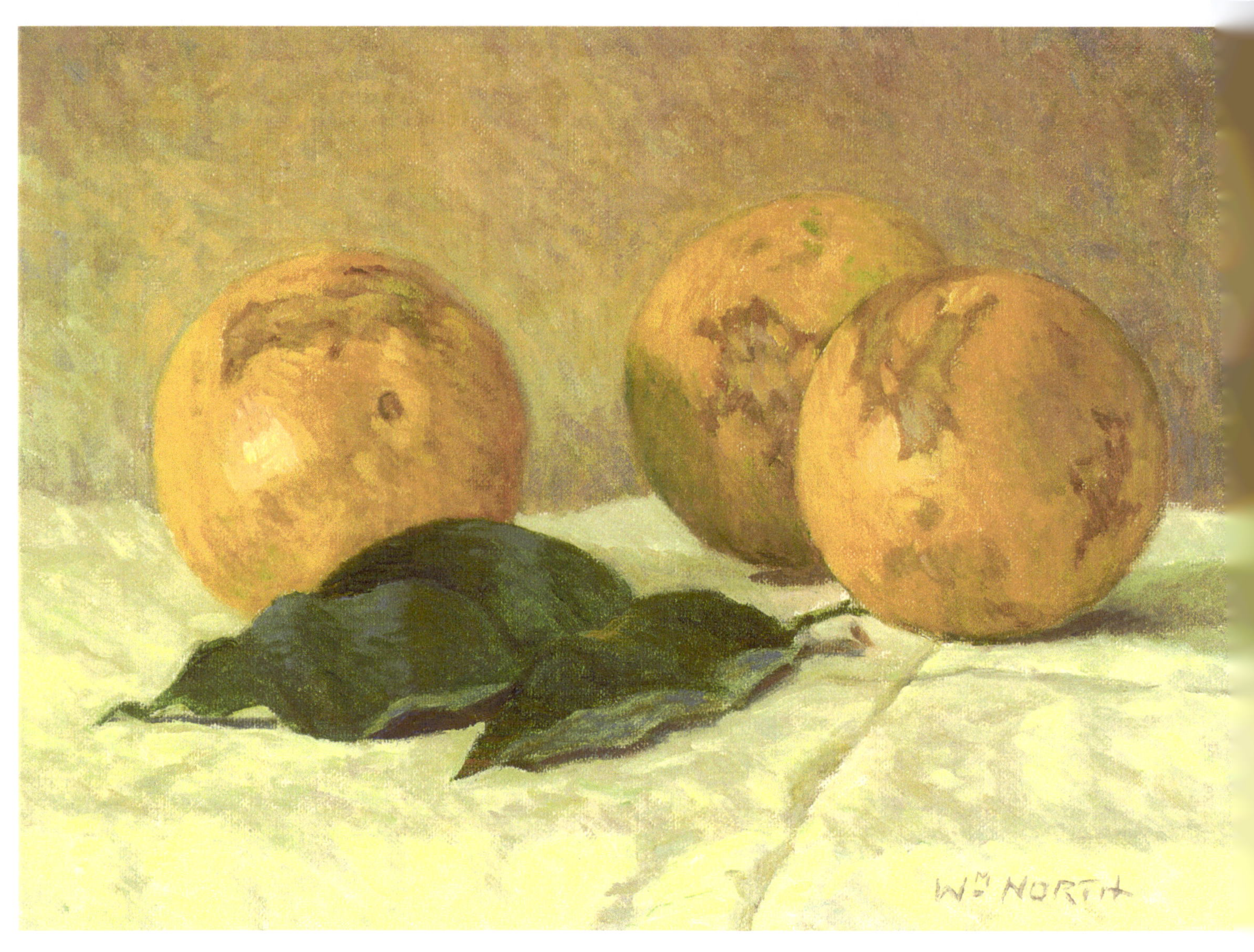

Valencias with Wind Scars, Florida Studio, Jun. 1998, 9" x 12"

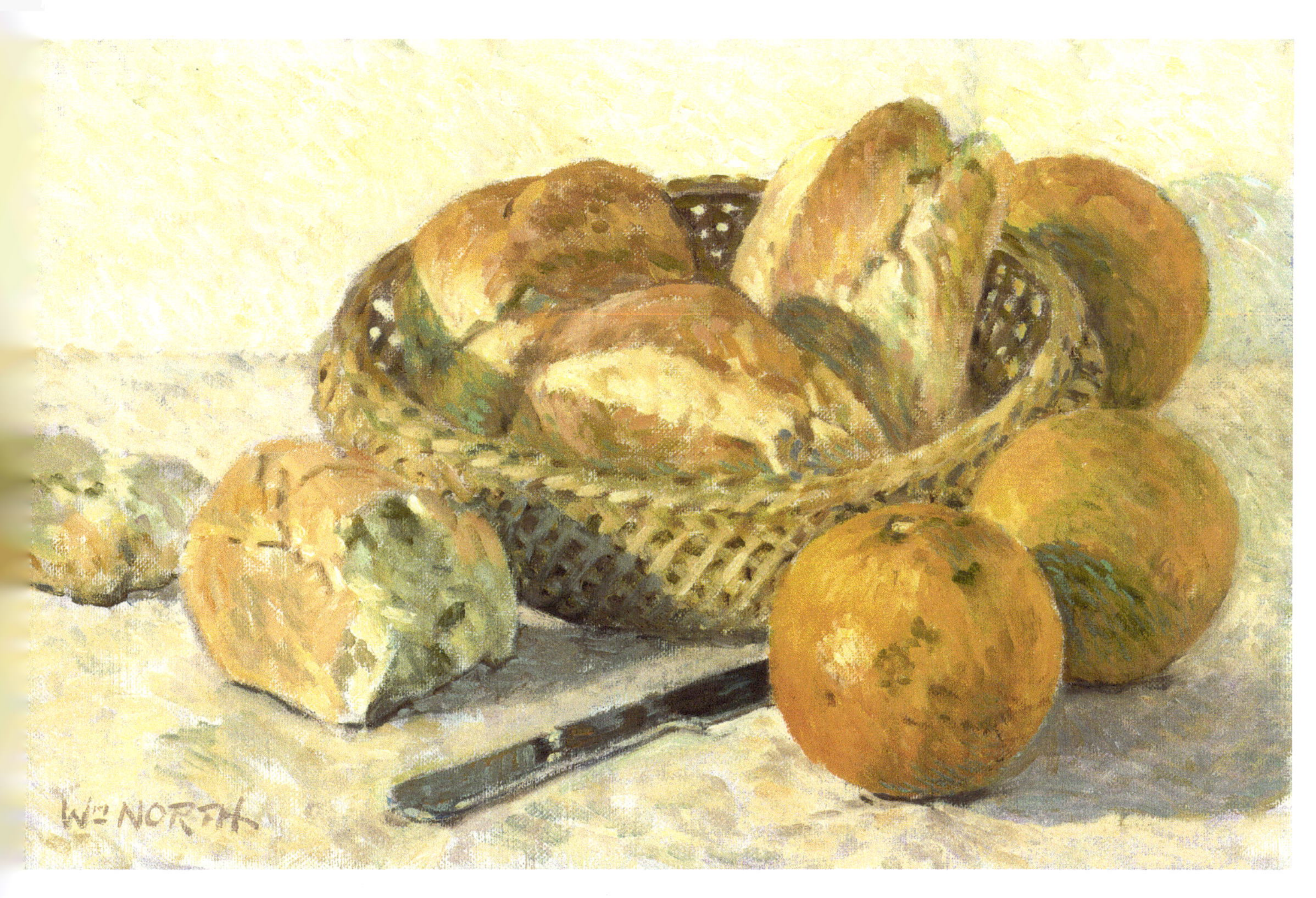

Florida Oranges, Chicago Rolls, Florida Studio, Jun. 1999, 9" x 12"

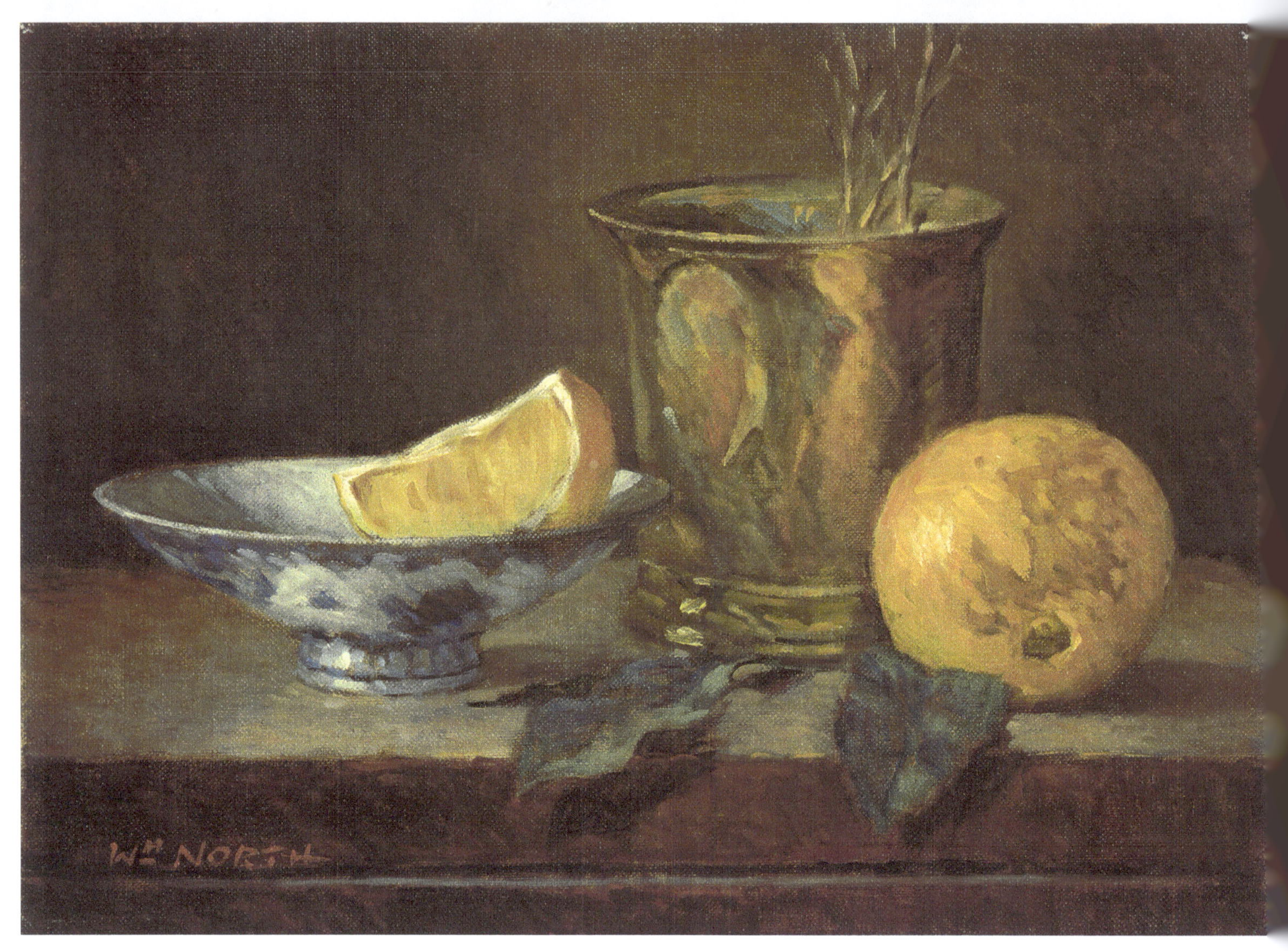

Valencia Reflections, Florida Studio, Dec. 1999, 9" x 12"

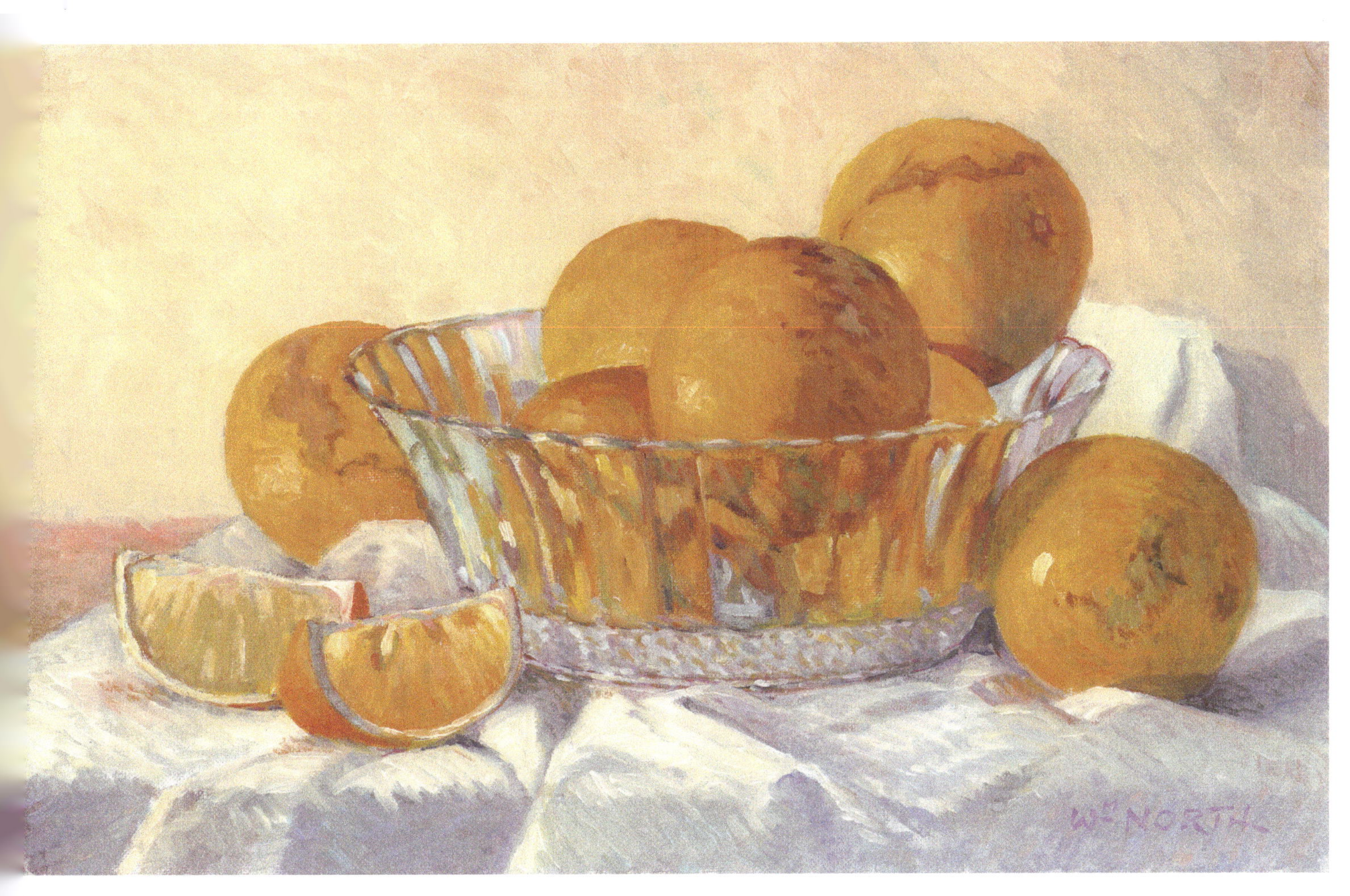

Golden Harvest, Florida Studio, Ft. Myers, FL, 9" x 14"

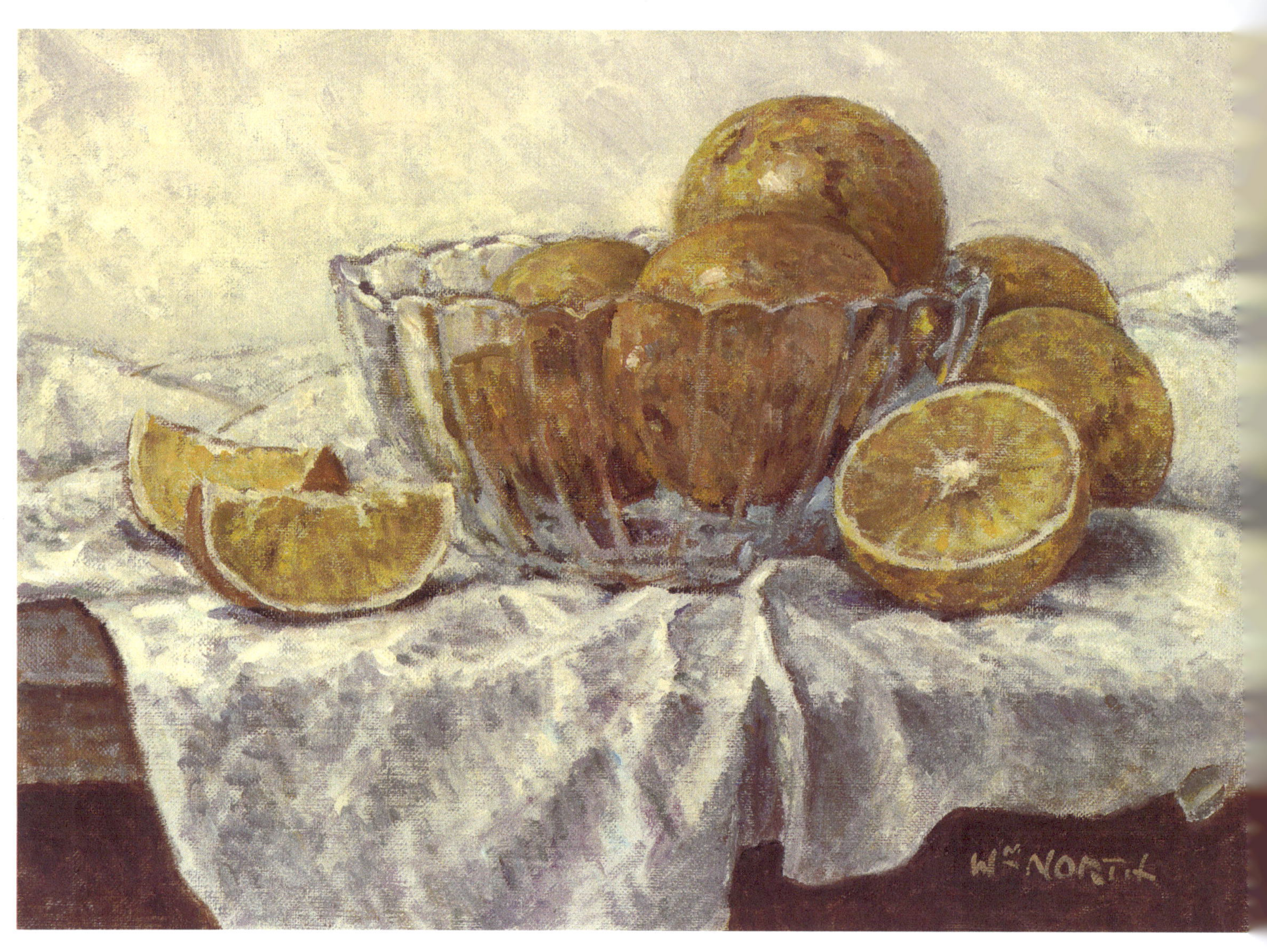

Red Valencias, Florida Studio, Mar. 2003, 9" x 12"

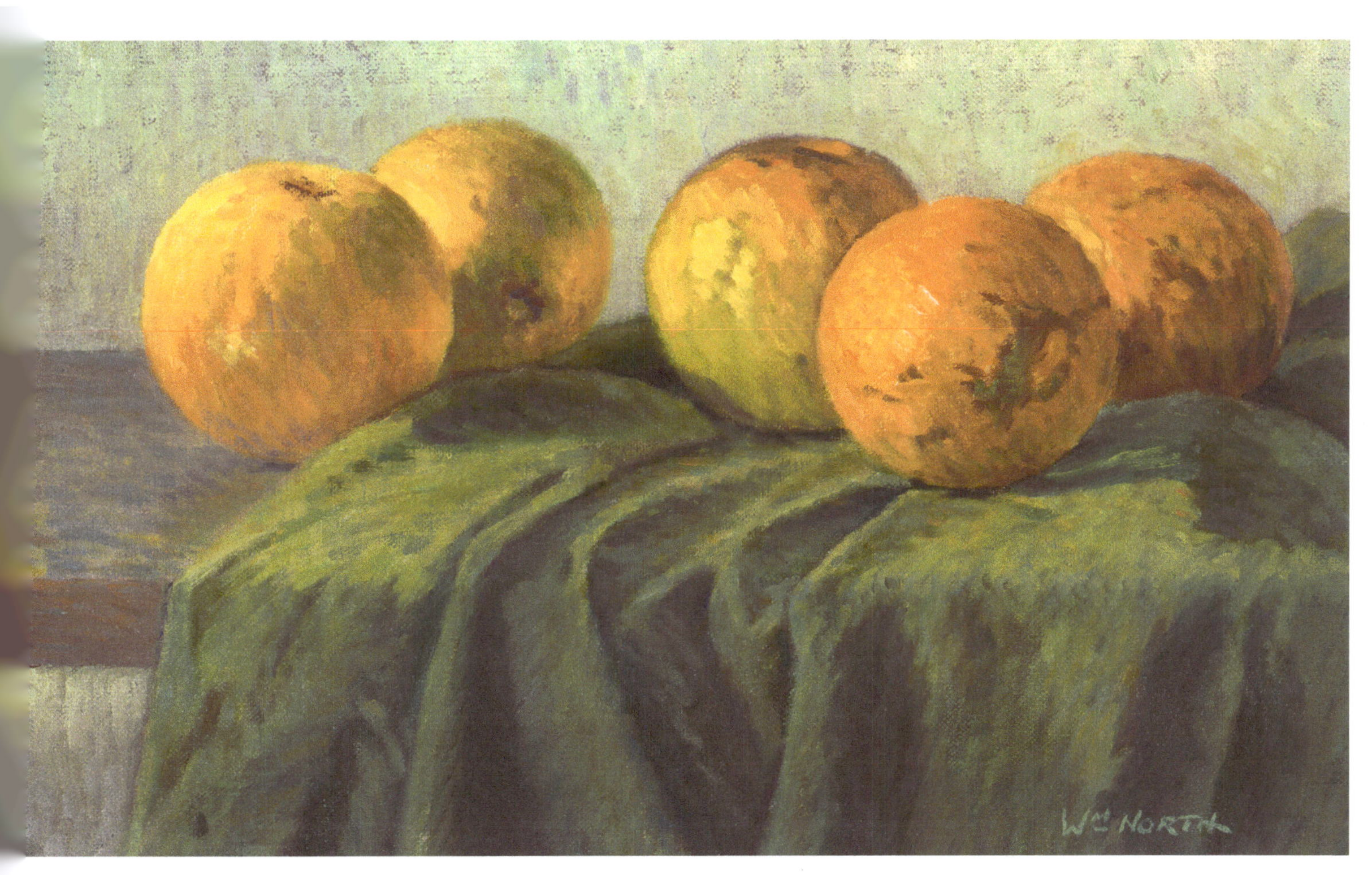

Five Florida Valencias, Florida Studio, Jun. 1999, 9" x 12"

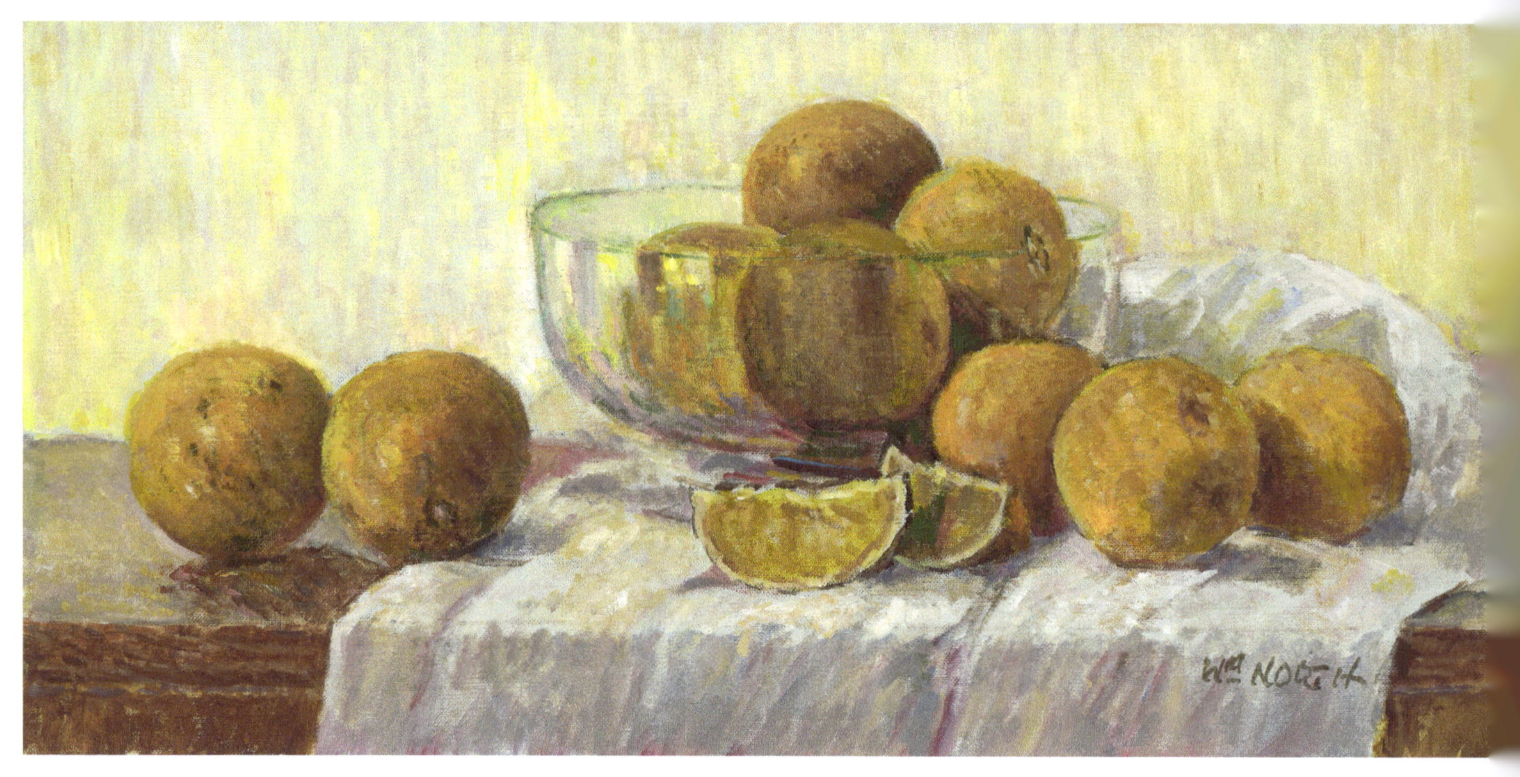

Florida Navels in Glass Bowl, Florida Studio, Aug. 2006, 10" x 20"

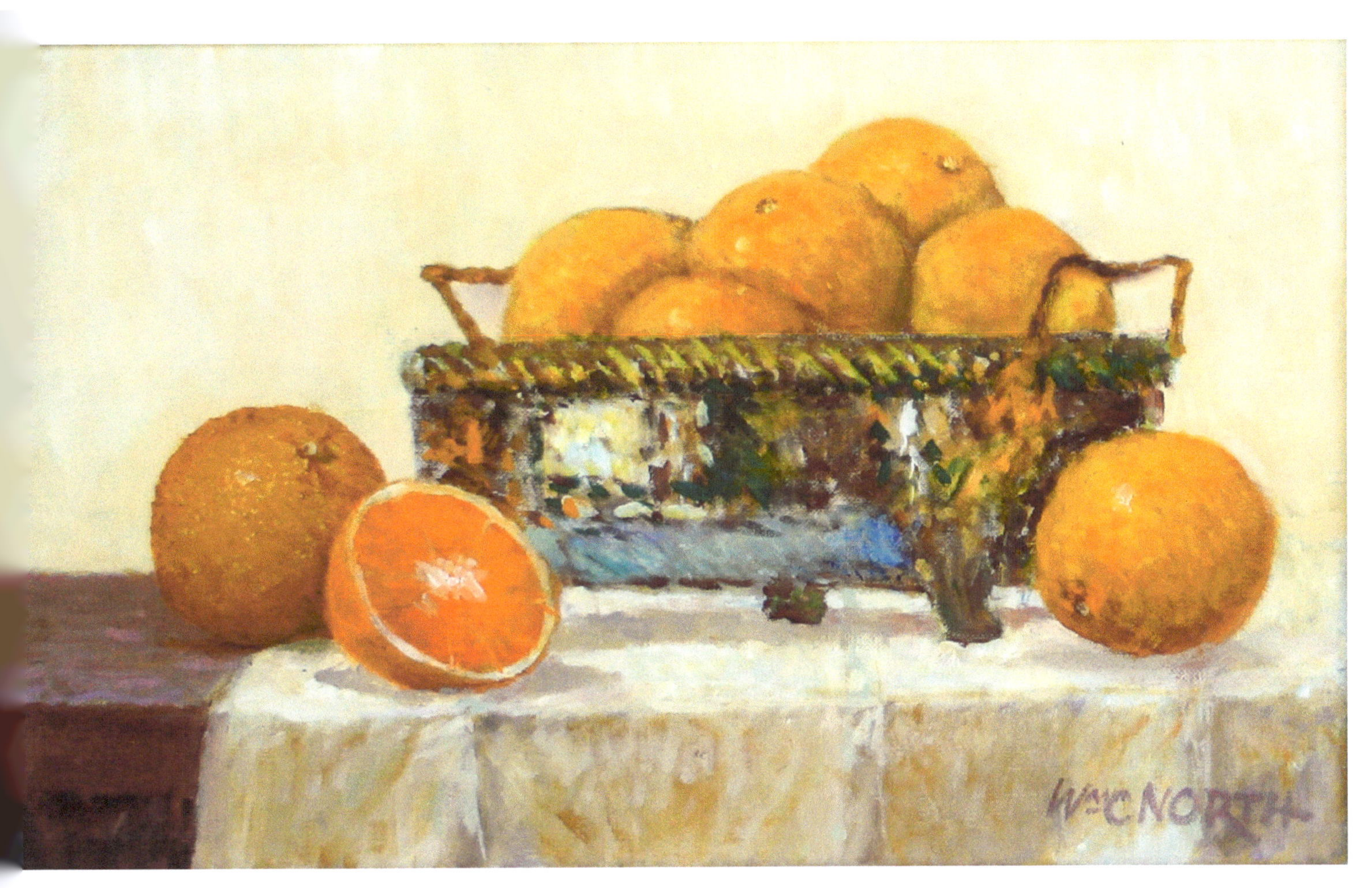

Fruit of the Season, Grand Court Studio, Ft. Myers, FL, 2010, 9" x 14"

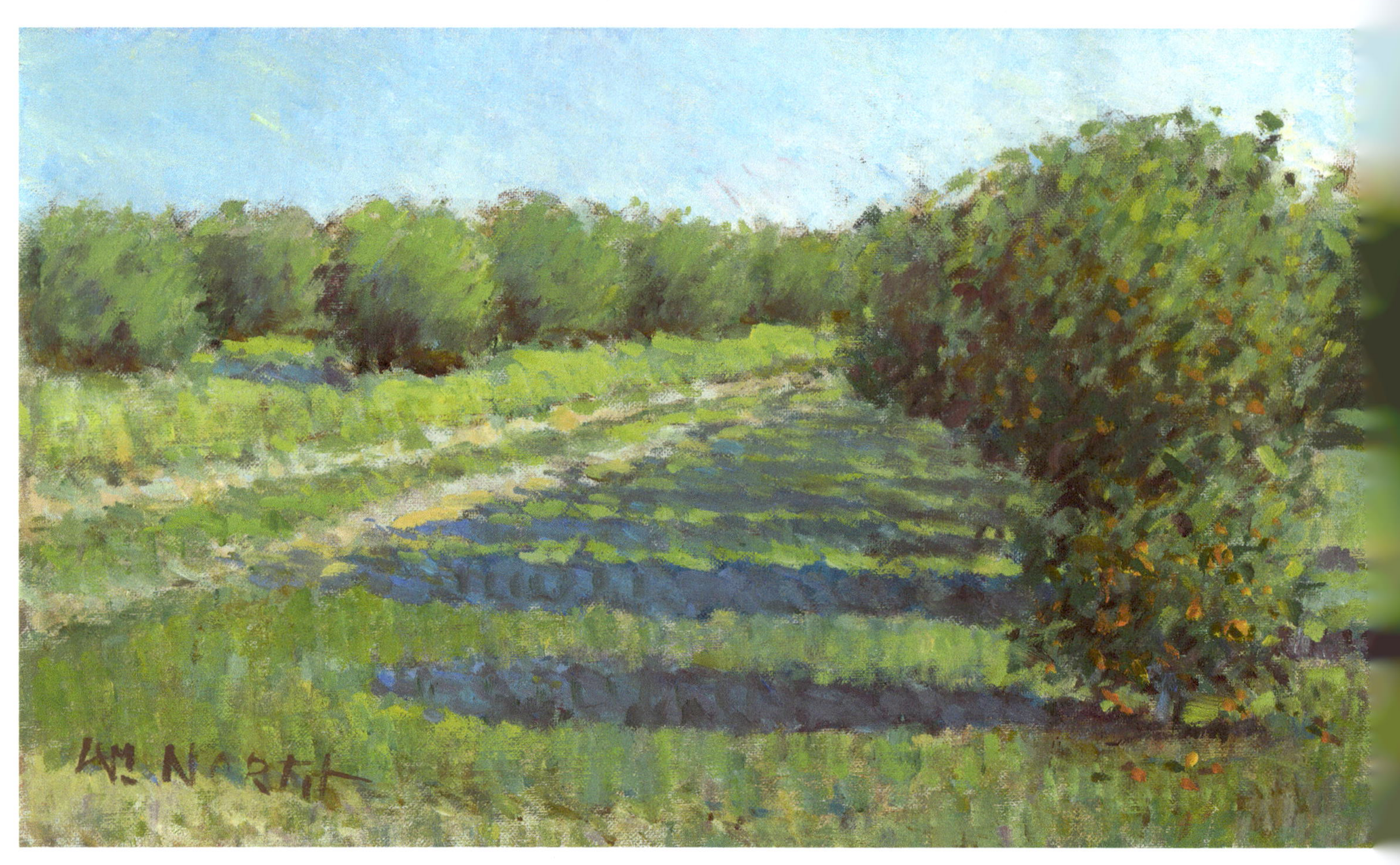

Florida Orange Grove #1, Mar. 2008, 9" x 14"

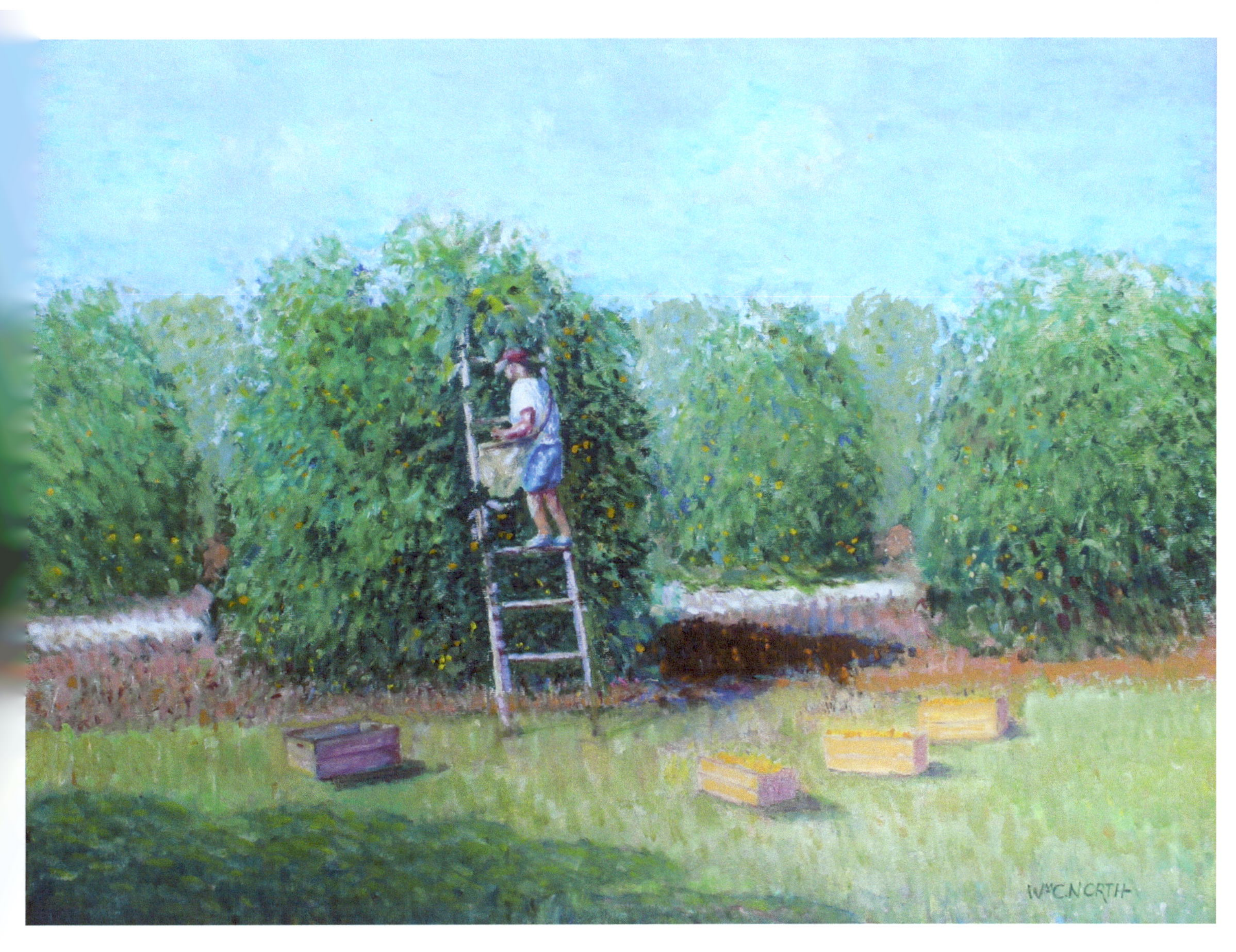

Hand Picking, Grand Court Studio, Ft. Myers, FL, Jan. 2011, 18" x 24"

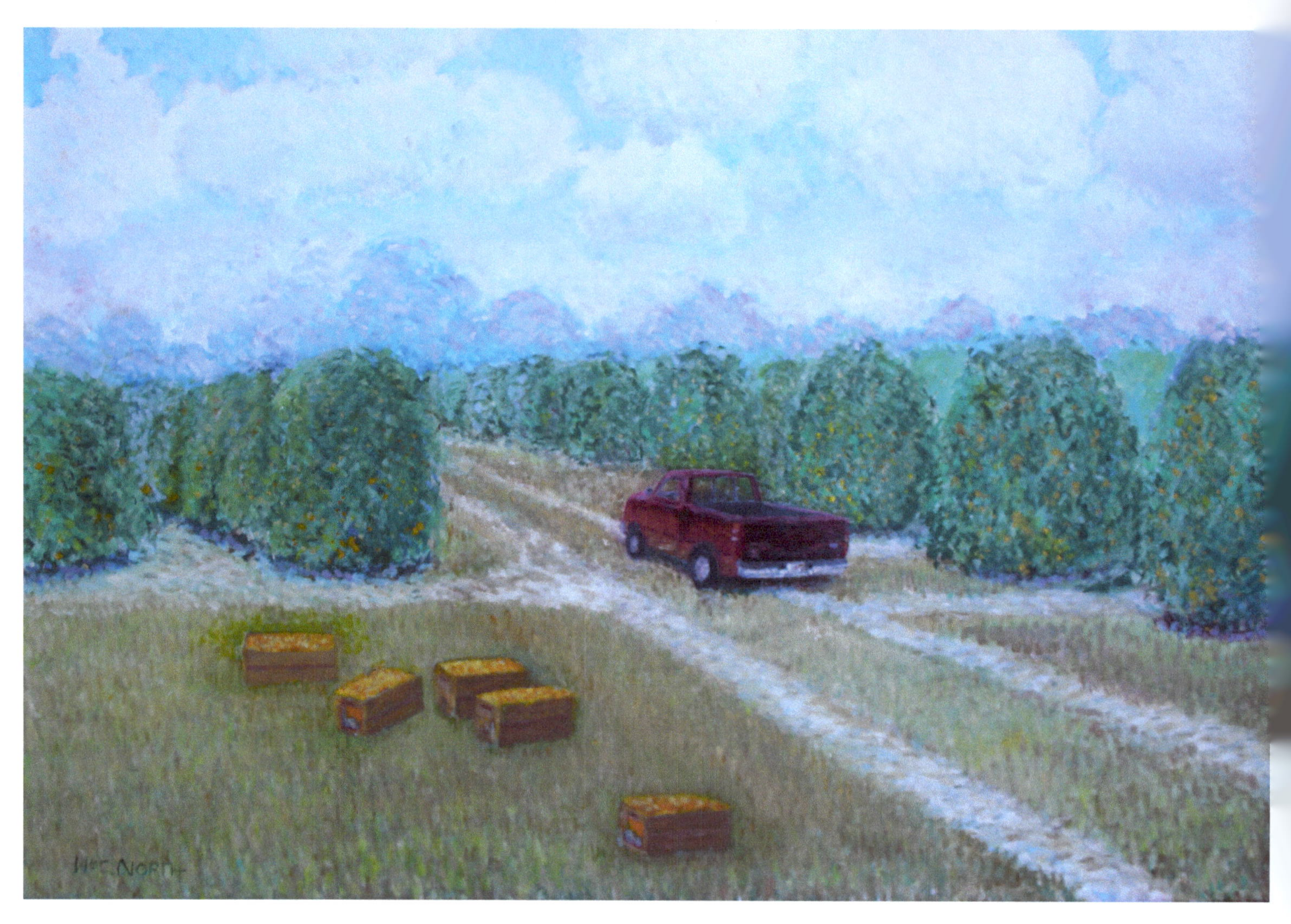

Red Truck, Grand Court Studio, Ft. Myers, FL, Jan. 2010, 24" x 36"

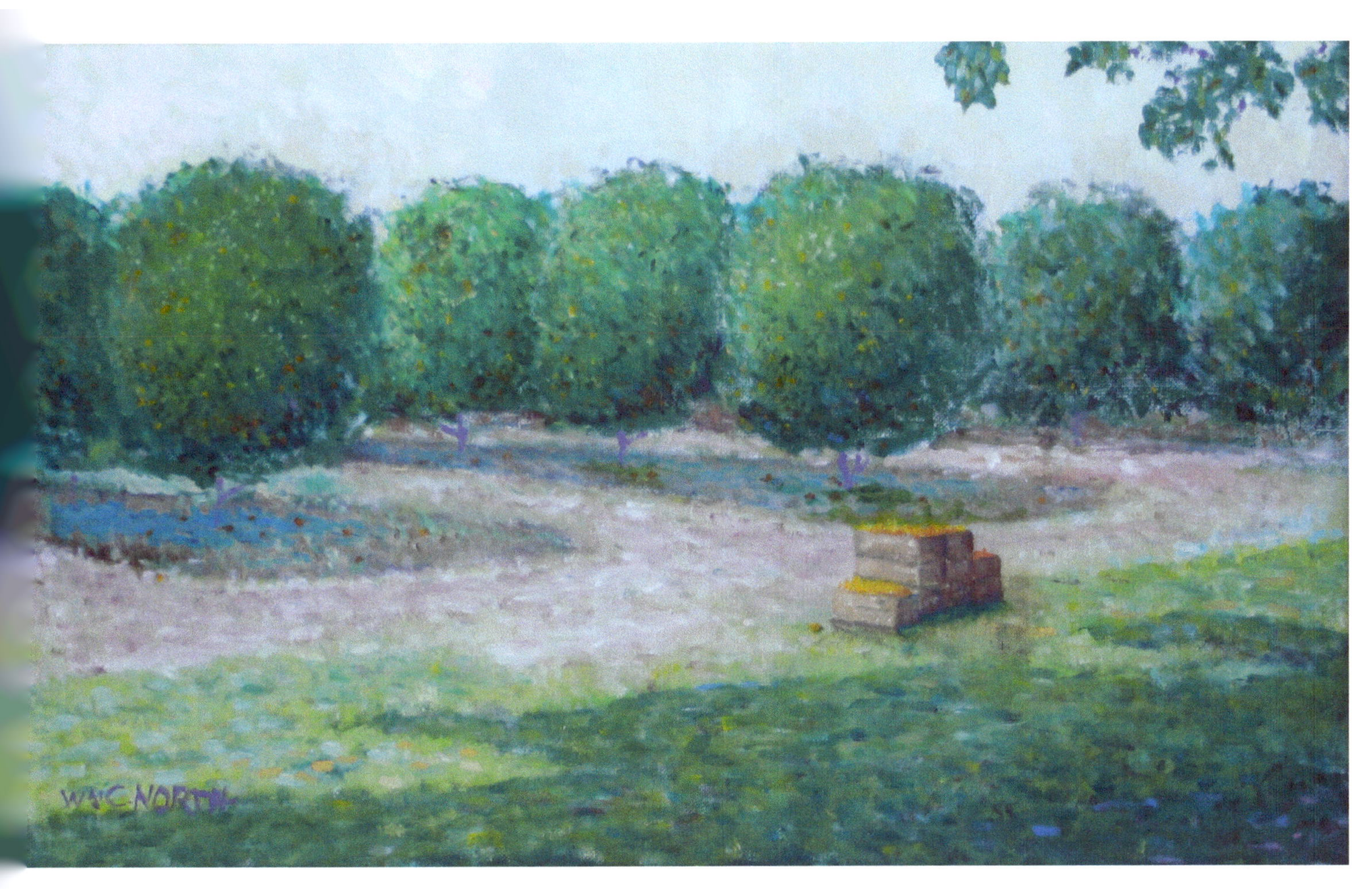

Stacked Crates, Grand Court Studio, Ft. Myers, FL, Dec. 2010, 10" x 16"

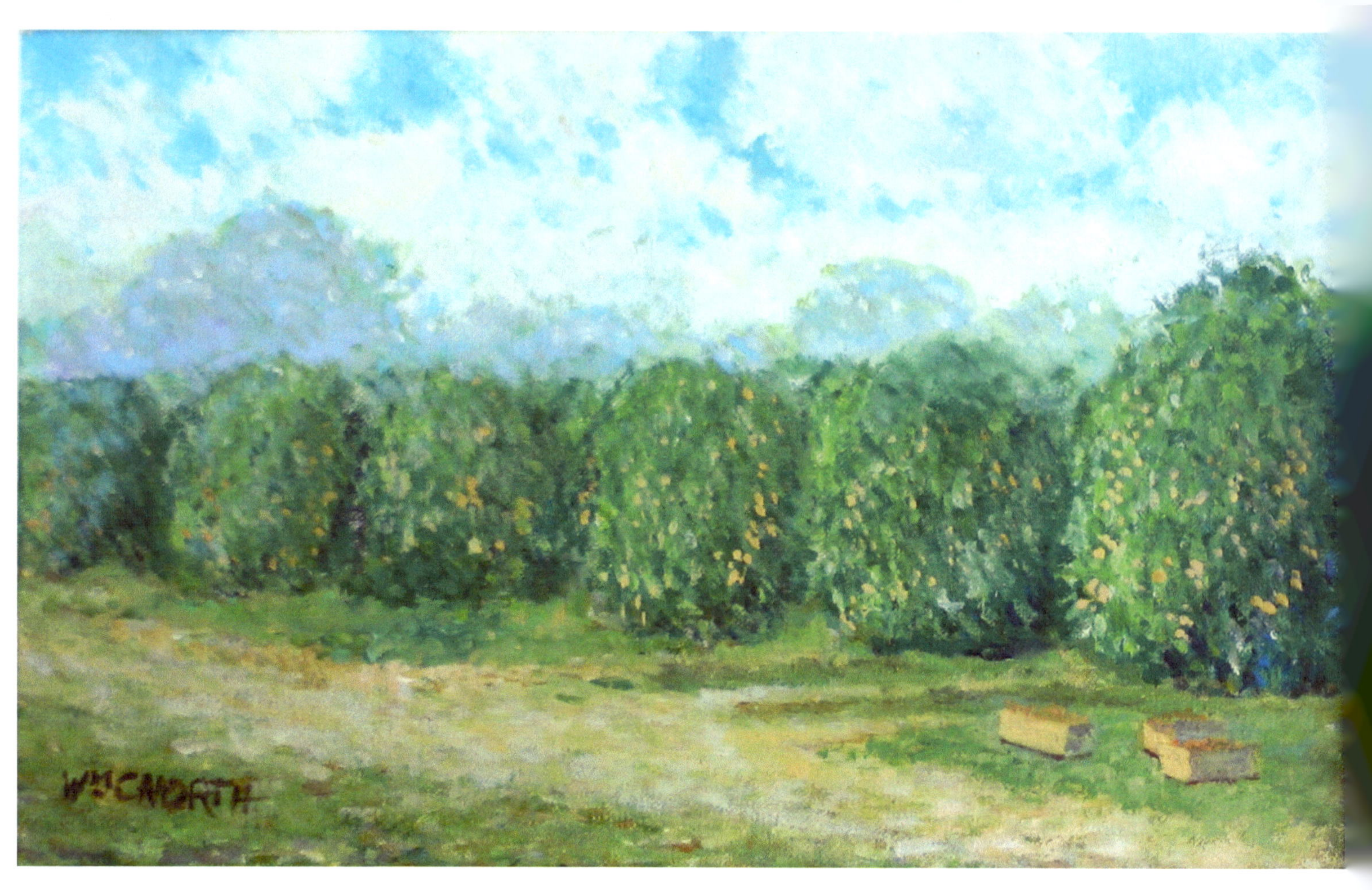

Orange Grove Road, Grand Court Studio, Ft. Myers, FL, Nov. 2010, 9" x 14"

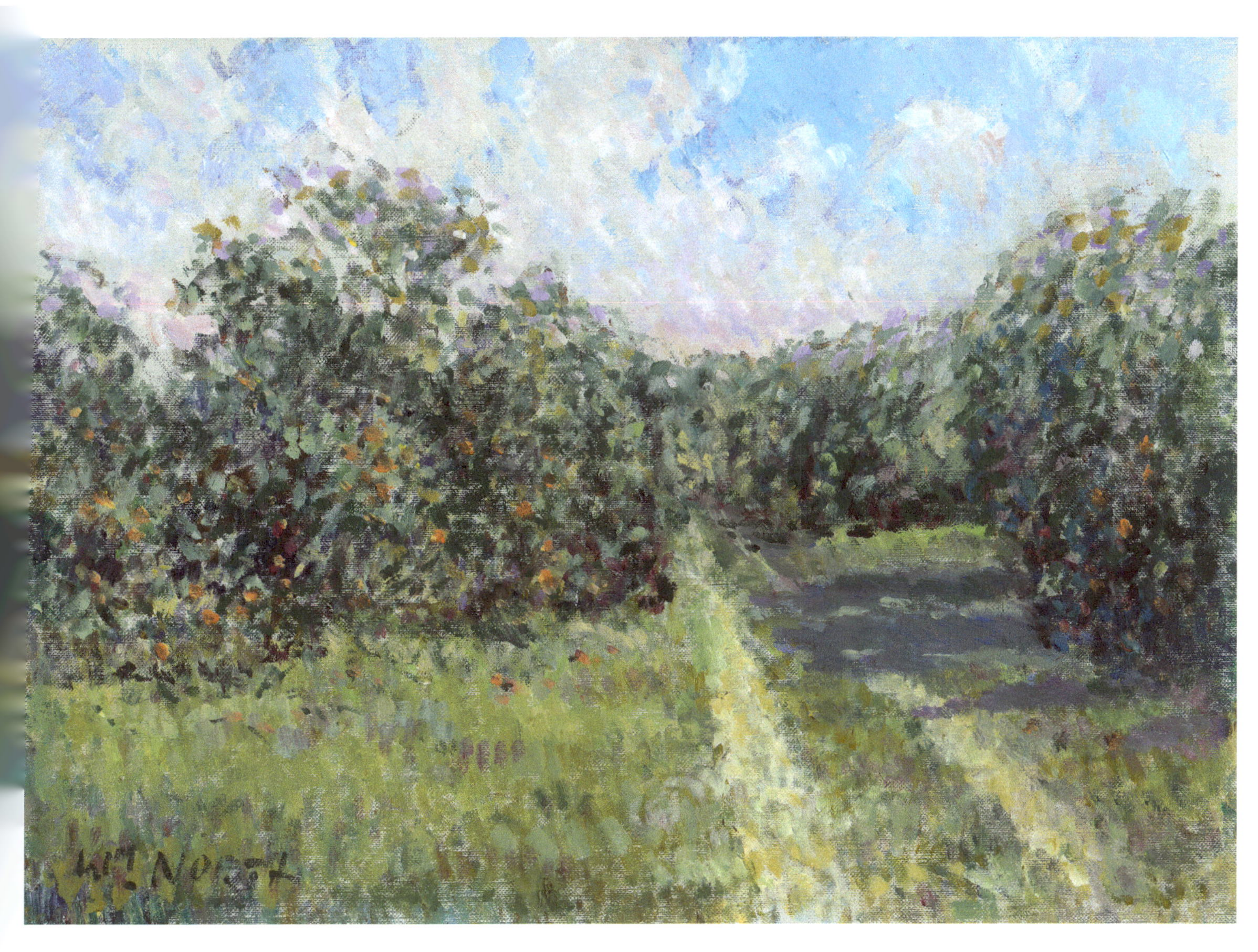

Florida Orange Grove #2, May 2008, 11" x 17"

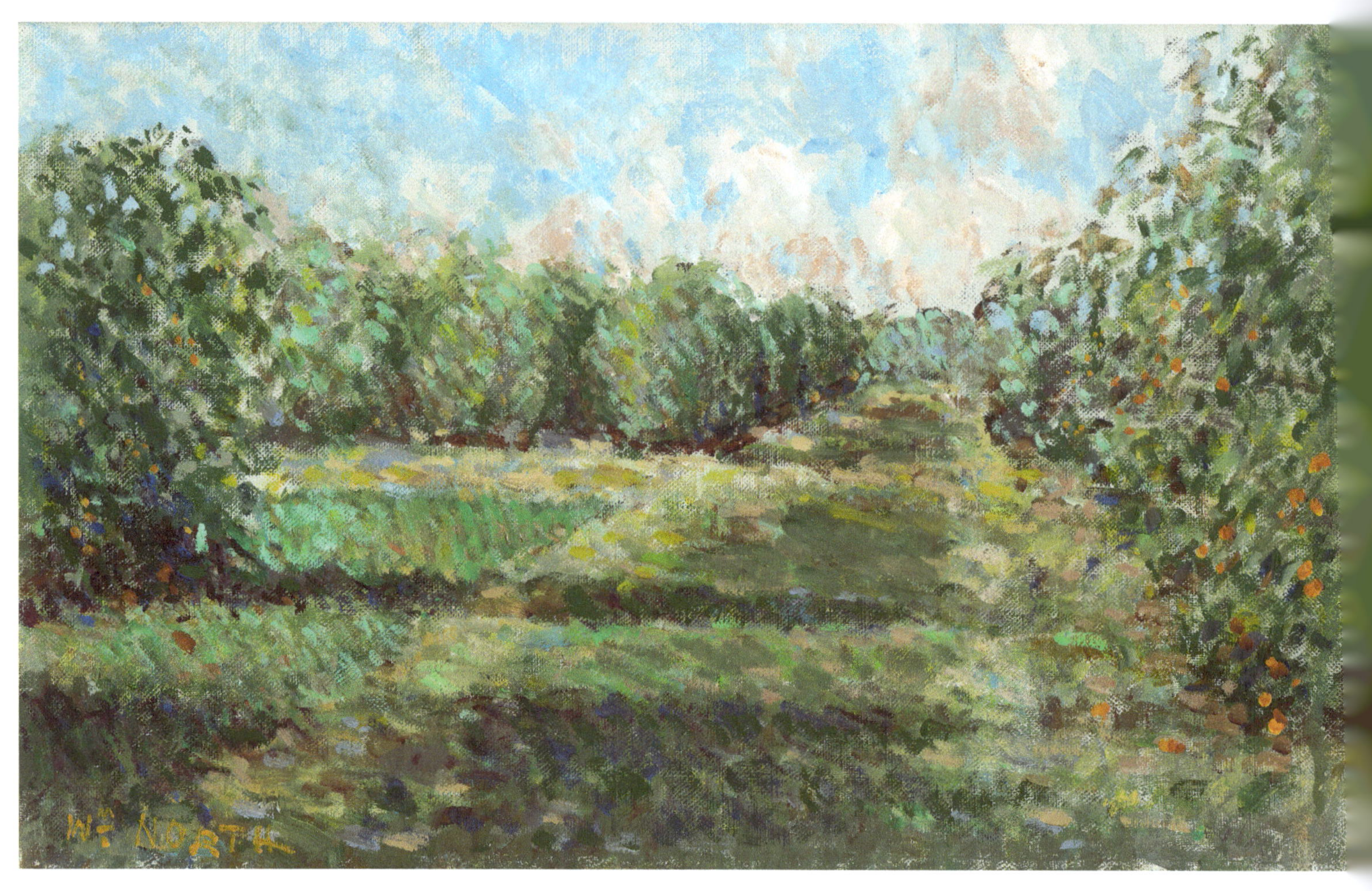

Florida Orange Grove #3, May 2008, 9" x 14"

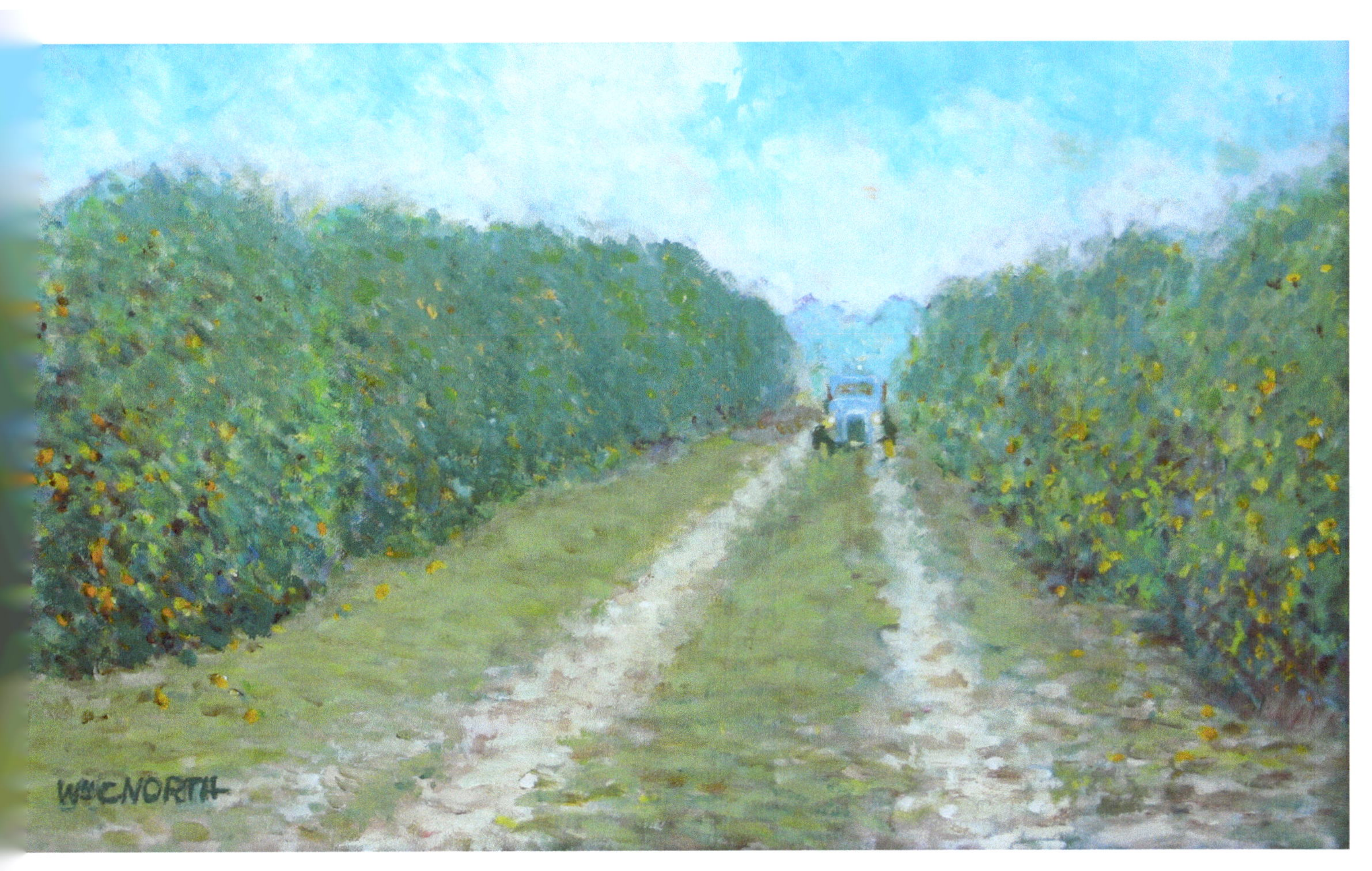

1937 Ford Truck, Ft. Myers, FL, Jan. 2011, 10" x 16"

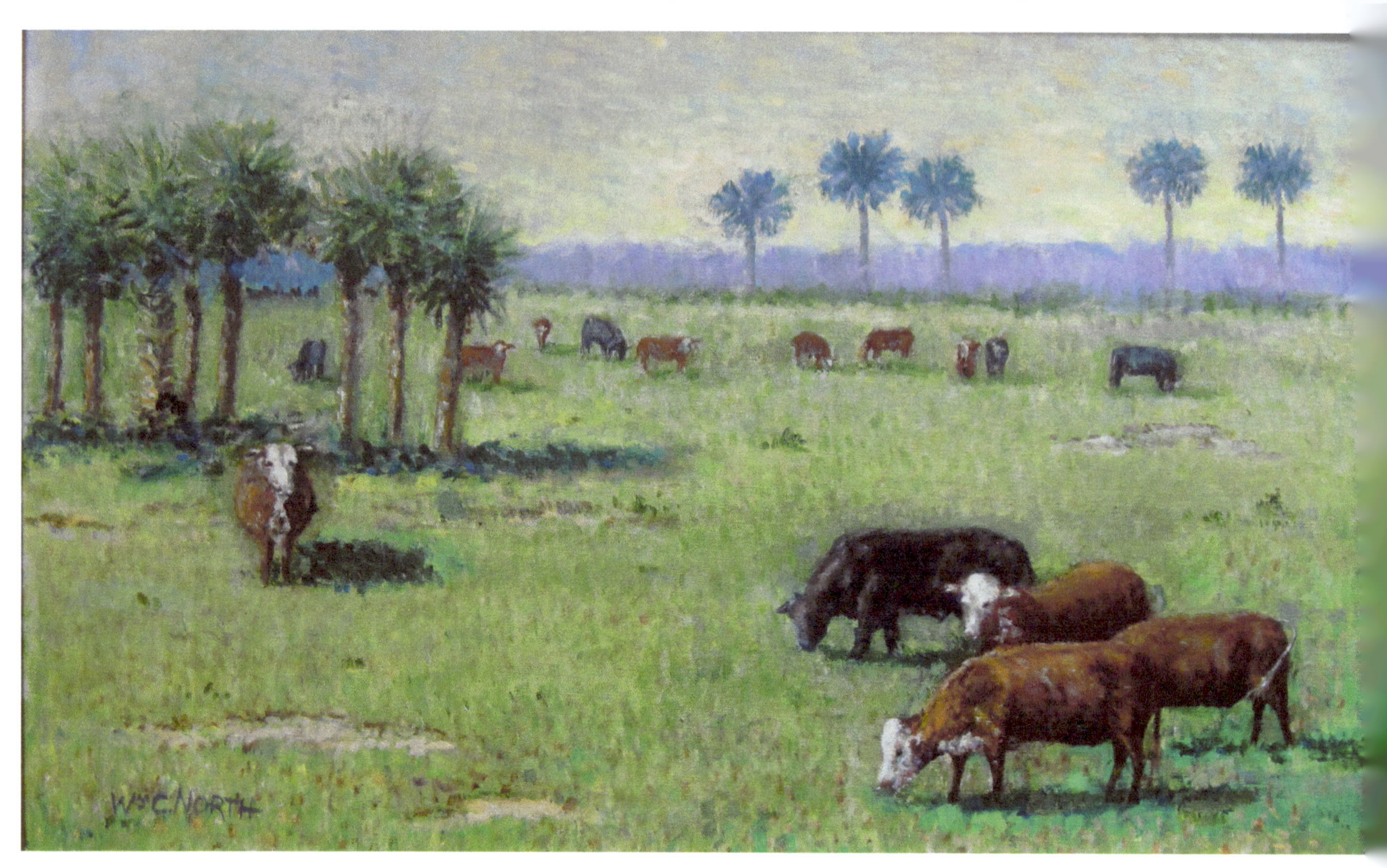

Florida Cattle Ranch, Grand Court Studio, Ft. Myers, FL, Oct. 2010, 14" x 22"

Afterword

A Life's Passion Realized

Colleen R. North

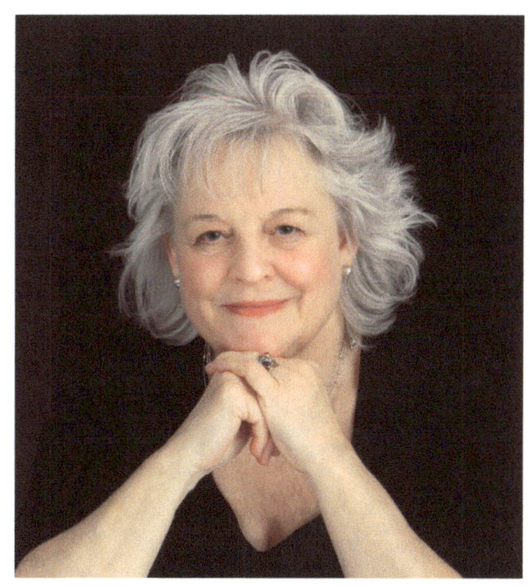

Although I've had a front row seat to most of my father's life, there's only so much a daughter can know about her father, particularly when you have not lived in the same house or even the same state for a few decades. Working with Dad on this memoir about his passion for painting has provided a special opportunity to learn more about him, and I'm thankful for the chance to help him put his life and his artwork between book covers.

Before this joint project, I never really understood that Dad felt he had led a double life: businessman by day, and artist at night and on weekends. It wasn't until he told me his stories that I realized how powerful a force his passion for painting has been throughout his entire life. Everyone in the family—my mother, my two siblings and I—were all happy for Dad when, after a fulfilling business life, and fitting his painting in when he could, in 1990 he could finally devote full time to painting. In the 20 years since, we have all been alternately amazed, surprised, and immensely proud to watch his professional artistic career take shape and flourish.

But the news we got in 2006 came as a shock.

While reading *The DaVinci Code*, Dad noticed a problem with his vision. Not one to make a fuss, it took a while to make an appointment with his ophthalmologist. An eye exam determined that he had macular degeneration, probably caused by years of painting outdoors in bright light. Dad's condition progressed very quickly from "dry" to "wet," creating the need for injection treatments to stabilize the condition, which he endured for several years. His family was not surprised at his courage during this time, and we've marveled at his ability to adjust his painting technique to keep up with these physical changes.

Dad's adaptations and achievements continue to inspire me. Entering his 80's, Dad also had to deal with glaucoma and cataracts, and finally his vision was such that he could not renew his driver's license. Fortunately Mom still drives, and some days, generous friends pitch in to deliver him home from the *Wm. North Gallery*. Although Dad's vision problems have hampered his painting and mobility, he continues to paint new oils and he has worked hard to develop new techniques for overcoming his disability so he can remain an active artist.

Dad's passion for painting drives him still, and I hope it always will. Whenever I visit, I find him in his efficient, cozy studio, working away. Two adaptations are that his canvases are larger and his impressionist style is somewhat looser. Hanging in his gallery, these newer paintings are hard to differentiate from paintings completed several years ago. If you ask Dad to critique his current works, he may lament the loss of some detail; however, his passion for the process comes shining through.

Recently he remarked, "Some say I'm painting better than ever."

I think he may be right.